CODING WITH PYTHON

50+ Practice Problems to Level Up Your Skills

THOMPSON CARTER

TABLE OF CONTENTS

INTRODUCTION

In a digital world driven by automation, data processing, and rapid information access, Command-Line Interface (CLI) applications are indispensable tools. CLI applications bring efficiency, flexibility, and power to both users and developers, enabling complex tasks to be performed directly from the command line, often in seconds and with just a few keystrokes. This book is a comprehensive guide to building robust, user-friendly CLI applications in Python, and it takes readers through every step required to create sophisticated, secure, and extensible CLI tools.

This book is written with a practical, hands-on approach, starting with the basics of setting up a CLI environment and culminating in a full-featured, multi-part project that synthesizes everything learned. Whether you are a software engineer, a data analyst, or a Python enthusiast looking to automate workflows, this book offers the tools, techniques, and best practices you'll need to build CLI applications that are reliable, efficient, and tailored to real-world use cases.

Why CLI Applications Matter

CLI applications may seem simple at first glance, but they serve as the backbone of many complex systems, powering everything from server management to software deployment, from data analysis pipelines to machine learning experiments. Unlike graphical user interfaces (GUIs), which require extensive design and often consume significant computing resources, CLI applications focus on functionality and speed. They are lightweight, scriptable, and easily integrated into other tools and workflows, making them an essential part of software infrastructure for many organizations.

With the rise of cloud computing, DevOps, and data science, the demand for powerful and flexible CLI applications has only increased. CLI tools provide the quickest way to interact with remote servers, automate repetitive tasks, and process large volumes of data. For developers, mastering CLI applications opens up a world of possibilities for optimizing daily tasks, scaling operations, and customizing workflows in highly efficient ways.

The Book's Approach

This book is structured around building both foundational knowledge and advanced skills, taking you step-by-step from the basics of CLI applications to the more complex features required for professional-grade tools. Every chapter introduces new concepts in a progressive manner, reinforcing them with practical examples, hands-on exercises, and a focus on best practices.

The book is divided into five main parts, each focusing on critical aspects of CLI application development:

1. **Fundamentals of CLI Applications**: We start with the basics—introducing CLI environments, Python's capabilities for handling command-line arguments, and building simple CLI commands. Readers will learn how to set up the development environment and implement straightforward commands, preparing them for more advanced functionality.

2. **Core Concepts and Data Handling**: Next, we dive into essential programming concepts like data structures, file handling, and input/output techniques. You'll learn to manage data effectively within CLI applications, from reading and saving files to implementing efficient data processing pipelines. These foundational skills are crucial for building applications that can handle and analyze data seamlessly.

3. **Advanced CLI Features**: In this part, we explore sophisticated features, such as user authentication, interactive menus, and error handling. By the end of this section, you'll have the knowledge to build CLI applications that are not only functional but also user-friendly, responsive, and secure.

4. **Project Challenges and Real-World Applications**: This section focuses on applying concepts to real-world

scenarios. Through projects like web scraping, data analysis, and automation tools, you'll put theory into practice, tackling challenges similar to those faced by professional developers. These projects are designed to demonstrate how CLI applications can solve actual problems and add value in practical settings.

5. **Capstone Project**: The final section brings everything together in a comprehensive capstone project. This multi-part project allows you to apply the skills you've developed throughout the book in a cohesive, realistic application that requires complex problem-solving, modular design, and user-oriented development.

Who This Book Is For

This book is designed for Python developers who are interested in building CLI applications that go beyond simple scripts and batch files. While some basic familiarity with Python is expected, each chapter is written to accommodate learners of varying skill levels. Concepts are explained with clarity and depth, providing enough context for beginners while also covering advanced techniques for experienced developers.

Specifically, this book is intended for:

- **Software Developers** looking to build reusable, modular CLI applications for automating tasks, managing infrastructure, or adding command-line features to their software.

- **Data Analysts and Data Scientists** who want to create command-line tools to preprocess, analyze, or visualize data, enhancing the automation of data workflows.

- **System Administrators and DevOps Engineers** who need powerful, flexible tools to manage servers, deployments, and infrastructure in cloud or on-premises environments.

- **Python Enthusiasts and Hobbyists** who want to explore the full capabilities of Python for building practical, effective applications outside the scope of GUIs.

By the end of this book, you will have a comprehensive understanding of how to design, develop, test, and deploy CLI applications. You'll be equipped with the tools and knowledge to:

- **Design User-Friendly CLI Interfaces**: Create intuitive, interactive command-line applications with structured menus, color-coded output, and progress indicators that enhance the user experience.

- **Implement Data Processing Pipelines**: Handle data efficiently within CLI applications, performing file operations, data parsing, and even basic analysis with libraries like pandas.

- **Build Robust, Secure Applications**: Incorporate user input validation, error handling, authentication, and secure data storage practices to build reliable CLI tools.
- **Extend CLI Functionality with Plugins**: Design applications with a plugin architecture, allowing users to add and customize features as needed.
- **Automate Testing and Deployment**: Use testing frameworks and Continuous Integration (CI) tools like GitHub Actions to ensure that CLI applications are reliable and easy to maintain.

Why Python?

Python is an ideal language for CLI applications, thanks to its simplicity, readability, and extensive library support. With modules like argparse, sys, and subprocess, Python natively supports CLI development, while libraries such as click and InquirerPy provide additional tools for building user-friendly and interactive command-line applications. Python's flexibility and strong ecosystem make it possible to integrate CLI applications with data processing, machine learning, cloud services, and much more.

Getting the Most Out of This Book

To maximize your learning experience, this book encourages you to:

- **Experiment with Code**: Each chapter contains code snippets and examples. Modify and experiment with these examples to better understand the underlying concepts.
- **Work Through the Projects**: The project-based approach is key to reinforcing concepts. Each project is designed to be achievable with what you've learned, yet challenging enough to stretch your skills.
- **Build and Customize Your Applications**: Once you've grasped the basics, take the initiative to extend the applications presented in the book with your own ideas and functionality.
- **Refer to Resources**: Many chapters introduce additional libraries, best practices, and resources for further reading. Use these resources to deepen your understanding and stay up-to-date with industry standards.

Building CLI applications is more than just writing scripts. It's about designing tools that are powerful, efficient, and accessible, enabling users to interact with data, manage systems, and automate tasks effortlessly. This book is your guide to creating CLI applications that are not only technically sound but also thoughtfully crafted for users.

Whether you're aiming to improve your productivity, automate repetitive tasks, or build powerful command-line tools for users, this book equips you with the knowledge and skills to accomplish your goals. So, let's dive in and start building CLI applications that make a meaningful impact.

CHAPTER 1: GETTING STARTED WITH PYTHON

Additional Key Topics Covered:

1. **Python Data Types and Variables**
   - Brief explanation of Python's main data types: integers, floats, strings, and booleans.
   - Introduction to variables: how to assign them, rules for naming them, and basic variable operations.
   - Examples to illustrate data types, such as storing a user's name as a string, age as an integer, and height as a float.

2. **Basic Mathematical Operations in Python**
   - Overview of arithmetic operators: addition (+), subtraction (-), multiplication (*), and division (/).
   - Introduce modulus (%), integer division (//), and exponentiation (**) operators.
   - Real-world applications for each operator.

3. **Using the input() Function**
   - Introduction to input() for collecting user input.
   - Converting input to different data types (e.g., int, float) to handle calculations.
   - Example: Ask the user for their age, convert it to an integer, and perform simple calculations.

4. **Comments and Code Documentation**

   ○ Explanation of single-line comments (#) and why they're essential for documenting code.

   ○ Introduction to multi-line comments using triple quotes (""" """) and their typical use in documentation.

Enhanced Real-World Examples

- **Basic BMI Calculator**: A program that takes a user's weight (kg) and height (m) and calculates their Body Mass Index (BMI). This example will introduce simple arithmetic, input handling, and variable assignments.

- **Simple Interest Calculator**: Write a program that calculates simple interest given the principal, rate, and time. This example demonstrates basic mathematical operations and user input.

- **Personal Budget Calculator**: A program where the user inputs their monthly income and expenses, calculates their balance, and gives feedback based on their savings vs. spending habits. This example uses basic arithmetic and if-statements to introduce conditional logic early.

Expanded Practice Problems

1. **Rectangle Area and Perimeter Calculator**:

○ **Problem**: Write a Python program that asks the user to enter the length and width of a rectangle and then calculates both the area and the perimeter.

○ **Skills Practiced**: Using variables, input() function, basic math, and print() for output.

2. **Time Conversion Program**:

○ **Problem**: Create a program that converts a given number of minutes into hours and minutes.

○ **Example**: If the user inputs 130, the output should be "2 hours and 10 minutes."

○ **Skills Practiced**: Integer division, modulus operator, and input handling.

3. **Tip Calculator with User Choices**:

○ **Problem**: Write a program that asks the user for the total bill amount and the tip percentage they'd like to give (e.g., 10%, 15%, 20%). The program should then calculate and display the tip and the total bill amount including the tip.

○ **Skills Practiced**: Basic arithmetic, variables, and user input.

4. **Unit Converter (Miles to Kilometers)**:

○ **Problem**: A simple program that converts miles to kilometers based on user input, with the conversion factor (1 mile = 1.60934 kilometers) provided in the code.

- o **Skills Practiced**: Variable assignment, multiplication, and input handling.
5. **Grocery List Calculator**:
   - o **Problem**: A program that allows users to enter prices of five grocery items, calculates the total, and displays it.
   - o **Skills Practiced**: Basic addition, handling multiple variables, and user input.

Bonus Mini Project: Interactive Story

As a way to practice user input and string handling, include a mini project where the program interacts with the user to create a simple story:

- **Problem**: The program prompts the user to enter words (e.g., a name, a place, an activity). These words are then used in a pre-written story template to create a unique story based on the user's input.
- **Skills Practiced**: String concatenation, variables, and input handling.

With this expanded chapter, readers will gain a deeper understanding of Python basics, covering data types, input, arithmetic, and program structuring while working on progressively more complex exercises. This foundational work will set them up for the chapters ahead by embedding a strong understanding of variables, user interaction, and output formatting.

CHAPTER 2: DATA TYPES AND

VARIABLES

In this chapter, we'll dive into Python's core data types and variables. We'll explore how to store and manipulate different types of information in Python, from simple numbers to text, through real-world examples. This chapter will build a strong foundation for handling data in Python.

Key Topics Covered:

1. **Introduction to Data Types in Python**
   - o Explanation of the fundamental data types:
     - **Integers**: Whole numbers without a decimal point (e.g., 42, -5).
     - **Floats**: Numbers with a decimal point, used for more precise values (e.g., 3.14, -0.01).
     - **Strings**: Text or characters enclosed in quotes (e.g., "Hello", 'World').
     - **Booleans**: Logical values True and False, used in decision-making.
2. **Understanding Variables and Assigning Values**
   - o Definition of variables as containers for storing data.
   - o Syntax for assigning values to variables with the = operator.

o Guidelines for naming variables, including best practices for readability (e.g., descriptive names, no special characters, use of underscores).

3. **Basic Operations with Different Data Types**

o Arithmetic operations on integers and floats: addition, subtraction, multiplication, division.

o Concatenation and repetition of strings using the + and * operators.

o Real-world applications for each operation, like performing calculations and combining strings for customized messages.

4. **Type Conversion**

o Converting between data types using functions like int(), float(), and str().

o Practical examples of type conversion, especially when taking user input (which is always a string) and converting it into a numerical format for calculations.

Real-World Examples

- **BMI Calculator (Enhanced)**: Expanding on the BMI calculator introduced earlier, this example now uses type conversion for user input, explaining how to convert string input into floats to calculate BMI.

- **Temperature Converter (Celsius to Fahrenheit)**: A program where users input a temperature in Celsius, which is converted to Fahrenheit using a formula. This example demonstrates both type conversion and basic arithmetic.
- **Simple Receipt Generator**: A program that stores the names and prices of a few items as variables, calculates a total, and prints a simple receipt message. This example uses integers, floats, and strings in a real-world scenario.

Practice Problems

1. **Basic Calculator**:
   - **Problem**: Write a program that asks for two numbers as inputs, performs addition, subtraction, multiplication, and division, and displays the results.
   - **Skills Practiced**: Variable assignment, arithmetic operations, and basic input handling.
2. **Age in Days**:
   - **Problem**: Ask the user for their age in years and calculate their age in days (assuming 365 days per year).
   - **Skills Practiced**: Integer operations, type conversion, and multiplication.
3. **String Formatter**:

- o **Problem**: Write a program that asks for a user's first and last name, then prints a message saying "Hello, [first name] [last name]!".
- o **Skills Practiced**: String concatenation, variables, and user input handling.

4. **Area of a Circle**:
   - o **Problem**: Create a program that asks for the radius of a circle, then calculates and prints the area using the formula $\pi * r^2$. Use 3.14159 as an approximation for π.
   - o **Skills Practiced**: Working with floats, exponentiation, and variable assignment.

5. **Trip Budget Calculator**:
   - o **Problem**: Write a program that asks the user for their budget for a trip, the cost of a hotel per night, and the number of nights they plan to stay. Calculate and print the remaining budget after the hotel cost.
   - o **Skills Practiced**: Basic arithmetic, variable assignment, and simple calculations.

Additional Mini Project: Personalized Story Generator

A program that takes multiple user inputs, such as name, favorite activity, and favorite color, and generates a personalized story using these variables. This is a fun way to practice using variables, string concatenation, and input handling.

Example:

- User inputs: name = "Alex," favorite activity = "hiking," favorite color = "blue."
- Output: "Once upon a time, Alex went on a fantastic blue adventure while hiking in the mountains!"

In this chapter, readers will gain hands-on experience with data types and variables, mastering how to store, manipulate, and convert data. By the end, they'll be comfortable handling basic data in Python, setting a strong foundation for more advanced programming concepts.

CHAPTER 3: BASIC INPUT AND OUTPUT

In this chapter, we'll explore how to interact with users through input and output, which is essential for creating interactive programs. Understanding how to gather user input, manipulate data, and format output will make your code dynamic and user-friendly.

Key Topics Covered:

1. **The input() Function**
   - **Basic Usage**: Introduction to the input() function for capturing user input.
   - **Prompts**: How to add a prompt message within input() to guide the user (e.g., input("Enter your name: ")).
   - **Handling Data Types**: Reminder that input() always returns a string, and how to convert this

input into integers, floats, or other types using functions like int(), float(), and str().

- o **Real-World Example**: Simple program that takes the user's age as input, converts it to an integer, and calculates how many years they have until retirement.

2. **The print() Function**

- o **Basic Output**: Introduction to print() for displaying messages to the user.

- o **Multiple Arguments in print()**: Using commas to print multiple arguments and how this adds spaces automatically.

- o **Concatenation in print()**: Combining strings with the + operator in print() statements.

- o **Real-World Example**: Personalized greeting program that takes the user's name as input and uses print() to greet them with a customized message.

3. **Formatted Output**

- o **String Formatting Techniques**:

  - ▪ **Old-style Formatting**: Using % for formatting strings (e.g., "Hello, %s!" % name).

  - ▪ **.format() Method**: Introduction to the str.format() method for inserting values into strings (e.g., "Hello, {}!".format(name)).

- **f-strings (Formatted String Literals)**: Python 3.6+ feature for formatting strings in a readable way (e.g., f"Hello, {name}!").

  o **Controlling Output Precision**: Formatting numbers to display a fixed number of decimal places.

  o **Alignment**: Adjusting text alignment within a formatted string (left, right, center) to make output clean and organized.

  o **Real-World Example**: Program to calculate the area of a circle and print the result with only two decimal places.

4. **Escape Characters and Special Formatting**

   o **Common Escape Characters**:

     - \n for a new line.
     - \t for a tab.

   o **Use Cases**: Creating multi-line messages, formatting output with tabs, and including special characters in strings (like quotes inside quotes).

   o **Real-World Example**: Simple receipt generator that displays items and prices in a tabbed format for readability.

Real-World Examples and Projects:

1. **Temperature Conversion Program**:

- Problem: Write a program that takes a temperature in Celsius, converts it to Fahrenheit, and displays the result in a formatted output.
- Skills Practiced: Input handling, type conversion, and formatted output.

2. **Simple Calculator with User Input**:
   - Problem: Build a calculator that asks the user to input two numbers and an operation (add, subtract, multiply, divide), then performs the operation and displays the result in a friendly format.
   - Skills Practiced: Using input() for multiple values, type conversion, and conditional logic.

3. **Loan Payment Calculator**:
   - Problem: Create a program that asks the user for loan principal, interest rate, and term length, then calculates and displays the monthly payment in a formatted message.
   - Skills Practiced: Input handling, mathematical operations, and formatted output for currency.

4. **Basic Quiz Program**:
   - Problem: A simple quiz program that asks the user a series of questions, takes their answers as input, and provides feedback at the end.

o **Skills Practiced**: Using input() to collect answers, conditional statements, and providing feedback with print().

5. **Personalized Daily Planner**:

   o **Problem**: Create a program that takes user input for their daily schedule (morning, afternoon, evening activities) and prints a nicely formatted schedule with timings.

   o **Skills Practiced**: Collecting multiple pieces of input, formatting output, and organizing text for readability.

6. **Currency Converter**:

   o **Problem**: Ask the user for an amount in their local currency and convert it to another currency using a predefined conversion rate. Display the result in a formatted manner.

   o **Skills Practiced**: Input handling, type conversion, arithmetic operations, and formatted output.

Expanded Practice Problems:

1. **Restaurant Bill Splitter**:

   o **Problem**: Ask the user for the total bill amount, the number of people, and the tip percentage. Calculate each person's share and display it in a formatted output.

- o **Skills Practiced**: Input handling, arithmetic calculations, formatted output.

2. **Shopping List Formatter**:
   - o **Problem**: Ask the user to input item names and prices, then print a shopping list with aligned names and prices for easy reading.
   - o **Skills Practiced**: Working with strings, formatted output, and organizing data in lists.

3. **Personalized Story Generator**:
   - o **Problem**: Take user inputs for several variables (name, place, activity, etc.) and create a short, funny story using these inputs with f-strings.
   - o **Skills Practiced**: String manipulation, using variables, and creative output.

4. **Multiplication Table Generator**:
   - o **Problem**: Ask the user for a number, then generate and display the multiplication table for that number up to 10.
   - o **Skills Practiced**: Looping (to be introduced if not yet covered), formatted output, and arithmetic operations.

Mini Project: Basic Interactive Game

Name: **Guess the Number**

- **Objective**: The program selects a random number between 1 and 100. The user has to guess the number based on hints provided by the program (e.g., "Too high" or "Too low").
- **Skills Practiced**: Input handling, output formatting, and simple conditional logic (though looping and random number generation might be introduced as a preview).

By the end of this chapter, readers will be skilled at gathering user input, converting data types as needed, and formatting output for readability. These skills are fundamental for making interactive and user-friendly Python applications.

CHAPTER 4: CONDITIONAL STATEMENTS

This chapter focuses on conditional statements, a fundamental concept in programming that allows the program to make decisions based on specific conditions. We'll explore if, elif, and else statements to help you build programs that can respond dynamically to different inputs and situations.

Key Topics Covered:

1. **Understanding Conditional Logic**
   - **Definition of Conditions**: Explaining conditions as expressions that evaluate to either True or False.
   - **Comparison Operators**: Overview of operators used to create conditions:
     - Equality (==)

- Inequality (!=)
- Greater than (>)
- Less than (<)
- Greater than or equal to (>=)
- Less than or equal to (<=)

o **Logical Operators**: Introducing logical operators to create complex conditions:

- **and**: True if both conditions are true.
- **or**: True if at least one condition is true.
- **not**: Inverts the truth value of a condition.

2. **The if Statement**

o Syntax and usage of the if statement to perform actions when a condition is True.

o **Basic Example**: Checking if a user is old enough to vote (age >= 18) and displaying an appropriate message.

o **Real-World Example**: Checking if an item is in stock and displaying a message to the user.

3. **The else Statement**

o Adding else to provide an alternative action when the if condition is False.

o **Basic Example**: Checking if a user is old enough to vote, with an else statement for users under 18.

o **Real-World Example**: Price discount scenario where customers get a discount if they spend above a certain amount; if not, they pay the regular price.

4. **The elif Statement**

   o Using elif for multiple conditions.

   o Explaining the sequential evaluation of conditions (Python checks each condition in order and stops once it finds a True condition).

   o **Basic Example**: Grading system where scores above 90 get an "A," scores between 80-89 get a "B," etc.

   o **Real-World Example**: Calculating shipping costs based on order total, with different rates for different price ranges.

5. **Nested Conditionals**

   o Introduction to nesting if statements inside each other.

   o **Basic Example**: A program that checks both age and membership status for a discount.

   o **Real-World Example**: Determining eligibility for different loan types based on income and credit score.

6. **Using Conditions with User Input**

   o Combining user input with conditional statements to create interactive programs.

o **Real-World Example**: Asking the user for their favorite color and responding with a unique message for each color.

Real-World Examples and Projects:

1. **Password Validator**:
   o **Problem**: Create a program that checks if a user's password meets specific criteria (e.g., length, inclusion of special characters).
   o **Skills Practiced**: if, else, elif, and logical operators.
2. **Temperature Advice Program**:
   o **Problem**: Write a program that takes the current temperature as input and provides advice based on the temperature range (e.g., "It's too cold," "Perfect weather," "It's hot").
   o **Skills Practiced**: elif statements and comparison operators.
3. **Basic Quiz Game**:
   o **Problem**: Design a simple quiz that asks multiple-choice questions and checks if the answers are correct.
   o **Skills Practiced**: if and else statements, with feedback based on the user's answers.

4. **Eligibility Checker**:
   - o **Problem**: Write a program that checks if a user is eligible for a specific offer based on their age, income level, and country of residence.
   - o **Skills Practiced**: Nested conditionals, logical operators, and comparison operators.

5. **Traffic Light Program**:
   - o **Problem**: Ask the user to input a color (red, yellow, green) and display a message based on the input (e.g., "Stop" for red, "Slow down" for yellow, "Go" for green).
   - o **Skills Practiced**: if, elif, and else statements.

Expanded Practice Problems:

1. **Even or Odd Checker**:
   - o **Problem**: Ask the user for a number and print if it is even or odd.
   - o **Skills Practiced**: Modulus operator and if statements.

2. **Number Guessing Game**:
   - o **Problem**: Have the program generate a random number, and the user has to guess it. Provide feedback on whether the guess was too high or too low.

- o **Skills Practiced**: Comparison operators, if statements, and logical thinking.

3. **Discount Calculator**:
   - o **Problem**: Ask the user for the total purchase amount. If it's over $100, give a 10% discount; if it's over $200, give a 20% discount; otherwise, no discount.
   - o **Skills Practiced**: elif statements and arithmetic operations.

4. **BMI Category Finder**:
   - o **Problem**: Ask the user for their weight and height, calculate BMI, and provide feedback (underweight, normal, overweight, etc.) based on BMI ranges.
   - o **Skills Practiced**: Arithmetic, conditional logic, and using multiple conditions.

5. **Event Ticket Price Calculator**:
   - o **Problem**: Create a program that calculates the ticket price for an event based on the user's age, with different prices for children, adults, and seniors.
   - o **Skills Practiced**: if, elif, and else statements with comparison operators.

Mini Project: Simple Banking System

Objective: Create a program that simulates a simple banking system, allowing users to check their balance, deposit, and withdraw money. It should check for sufficient funds before allowing a withdrawal.

- **Problem Breakdown**:
  - Prompt the user for their starting balance.
  - Offer options to:
    - **Check Balance**: Display the current balance.
    - **Deposit**: Ask for an amount and add it to the balance.
    - **Withdraw**: Ask for an amount and subtract it from the balance only if there are enough funds.
  - Use if, elif, and else statements to manage each action.
  - **Skills Practiced**: Nested conditionals, user input, basic arithmetic, and decision-making.

This chapter introduces conditional statements, empowering readers to build programs that can make decisions based on different scenarios. By the end, readers will be able to use if, elif, and else to create more dynamic and interactive Python applications.

CHAPTER 5: LOOPS AND ITERATION

This chapter focuses on loops, a crucial feature in programming that allows you to execute repetitive tasks efficiently. We'll cover for and while loops, along with nested loops and some practical exercises to solidify your understanding.

Key Topics Covered:

1. **Introduction to Loops**
   - **Definition and Purpose**: Why loops are essential for repeating tasks and reducing code redundancy.

- o **Types of Loops in Python**: Overview of for loops and while loops and when to use each.

2. **The for Loop**

   - o **Basic Syntax**: Understanding the for loop structure, including the loop variable and iteration over sequences.
   - o **Using range()**: Exploring the range() function to create sequences for loop iteration.
     - Examples with range(start, stop) and range(start, stop, step).
   - o **Looping through Collections**: How to use for loops to iterate over lists, tuples, and strings.
   - o **Real-World Example**: Displaying a countdown or generating a list of even numbers.

3. **The while Loop**

   - o **Basic Syntax**: Structure of a while loop, which continues as long as a specified condition is True.
   - o **Infinite Loops and Exit Conditions**: How to control loop execution to avoid infinite loops and why while True is sometimes useful with proper exit conditions.
   - o **Real-World Example**: A simple program that repeatedly asks the user for a password until they provide the correct one.

4. **Nested Loops**

o **Definition and Use Cases**: When and why to use loops inside loops, such as in matrix operations or multi-dimensional data processing.

o **Real-World Example**: Printing a multiplication table using nested loops.

5. **Control Statements**

o **break Statement**: How to exit a loop early when a certain condition is met.

o **continue Statement**: Skipping the current iteration and moving to the next one.

o **pass Statement**: Placeholder statement for unimplemented code.

o **Real-World Example**: A number guessing game where the loop breaks once the correct answer is guessed.

Real-World Examples and Projects

1. **Number Summation Program**:

o **Problem**: Write a program that calculates the sum of all numbers from 1 to a user-specified limit using a for loop.

o **Skills Practiced**: for loops, range(), and basic arithmetic.

2. **Factorial Calculator**:

   o **Problem**: Create a program that calculates the factorial of a number entered by the user using a while loop.

   o **Skills Practiced**: while loops and handling user input.

3. **Password Checker with Limited Attempts**:

   o **Problem**: Write a program that asks for a password, allowing only three attempts before locking the user out.

   o **Skills Practiced**: while loop with an exit condition, if statements, and tracking attempts.

4. **Multiplication Table Generator**:

   o **Problem**: Create a program that generates and displays the multiplication table for numbers 1 to 10 using nested loops.

   o **Skills Practiced**: Nested for loops and formatted output.

5. **Prime Number Checker**:

   o **Problem**: Ask the user for a number and check if it is prime using a for loop.

   o **Skills Practiced**: for loop, conditional statements, and modulus operator.

6. **User Menu with Looping**:

- o **Problem**: Write a program that displays a menu to the user with options to check balance, deposit, withdraw, and exit. Use a loop to keep showing the menu until the user chooses to exit.
- o **Skills Practiced**: while loop, if statements, and interactive user input.

Expanded Practice Problems

1. **Average Calculator**:
   - o **Problem**: Write a program that repeatedly asks for numbers, calculates the average, and stops when the user enters a specific value (e.g., -1).
   - o **Skills Practiced**: while loop, input handling, and arithmetic operations.
2. **Fibonacci Sequence Generator**:
   - o **Problem**: Use a for loop to generate the first n terms of the Fibonacci sequence, where n is provided by the user.
   - o **Skills Practiced**: for loops, basic arithmetic, and sequence generation.
3. **Letter Frequency Counter**:
   - o **Problem**: Ask the user for a word or sentence, and use a for loop to count the frequency of each letter.
   - o **Skills Practiced**: for loop, string manipulation, and dictionary data structure (for storing counts).

4. **Simple Game: Rock, Paper, Scissors**:

   o **Problem**: Create a game where the user plays rock-paper-scissors against the computer in a loop. The game should continue until the user decides to stop.

   o **Skills Practiced**: while loop, random number generation, and conditional statements.

5. **Temperature Conversion Table**:

   o **Problem**: Write a program that generates a table of Celsius temperatures and their Fahrenheit equivalents from 0 to 100 degrees in increments of 10.

   o **Skills Practiced**: for loop, formatted output, and arithmetic.

Mini Project: Simple Quiz Program

Objective: Create a multiple-choice quiz program with 5-10 questions. The user answers each question, and the program keeps track of correct answers. At the end, display the total score.

- **Problem Breakdown**:

   o Create a list of questions, each with possible answers.

   o Use a for loop to iterate over each question, displaying it and asking for user input.

○ Check if the user's answer is correct and update the score accordingly.

○ Display the final score after the quiz is complete.

○ **Skills Practiced**: for loops, lists, conditional statements, and user input.

This chapter equips readers with the skills to handle repetitive tasks effectively in Python, covering for and while loops, nested loops, and control statements. By the end of this chapter, readers will be able to use loops to handle a wide range of practical scenarios, from simple counters to complex nested operations.

CHAPTER 6: FUNCTIONS AND MODULAR CODE

Functions are the building blocks of modular code, enabling you to write reusable, organized, and efficient code. In this chapter, we'll cover how to create functions, pass arguments, use return values, and apply best practices for modular programming.

Key Topics Covered:

1. **Introduction to Functions**

o **What is a Function?**: Explanation of functions as reusable blocks of code that perform specific tasks.

o **Benefits of Functions**: Modularity, reusability, and the ability to break down complex problems into simpler, manageable tasks.

o **Basic Syntax**: The structure of defining a function in Python using the def keyword, function name, parentheses, and a colon (:).

2. **Creating a Basic Function**

o **Defining and Calling Functions**: Step-by-step example of defining a function and calling it to execute.

o **Example**: Writing a function that prints a greeting message, then calling it multiple times.

3. **Function Parameters and Arguments**

o **Parameters and Arguments**: Explanation of parameters as placeholders and arguments as the actual values passed to functions.

o **Positional Arguments**: Understanding how arguments are passed based on their position.

o **Keyword Arguments**: Using keywords to specify arguments by name, allowing flexibility in argument order.

- o **Default Parameter Values**: Setting default values for parameters, allowing functions to be called with fewer arguments.
- o **Example**: Writing a function that calculates the area of a rectangle, with a default value for the width.

4. **Return Values**
   - o **The return Statement**: Using return to send back a value from a function to where it was called.
   - o **Return vs. Print**: Difference between returning a value and printing it, emphasizing why returning values is often more useful for modularity.
   - o **Multiple Return Values**: Returning multiple values as a tuple.
   - o **Example**: Writing a function that calculates the area and perimeter of a rectangle and returns both values.

5. **Scope and Lifetime of Variables**
   - o **Local and Global Variables**: Explanation of variable scope, with a focus on the fact that variables defined inside functions are local and not accessible outside.
   - o **Using global Keyword**: Brief explanation of the global keyword and why it should be used cautiously.

- o **Example**: Demonstrating scope by creating a function that modifies a local variable, showing how it doesn't affect variables outside the function.

6. **Modular Code with Functions**

- o **Organizing Code**: Using functions to divide programs into modules, each handling a specific task.

- o **Reusability and Readability**: Emphasis on how functions make code easier to understand, maintain, and reuse.

- o **Example**: Refactoring a longer program into multiple functions, each responsible for a distinct part of the task.

Real-World Examples and Projects:

1. **Temperature Converter Function**:

- o **Problem**: Write a function that converts temperatures from Celsius to Fahrenheit and another that converts from Fahrenheit to Celsius.

- o **Skills Practiced**: Defining functions, parameters, and return values.

2. **Shopping Cart Calculator**:

- o **Problem**: Create a function that takes a list of item prices, calculates the total price, and returns it.
- o **Skills Practiced**: Function parameters, loops (to iterate over the list), and return values.

3. **Basic Calculator with Functions**:
   - o **Problem**: Write separate functions for addition, subtraction, multiplication, and division. Then create a main function that calls these based on user input.
   - o **Skills Practiced**: Using functions as modules, parameters, return values, and conditional statements.

4. **Factorial Calculator**:
   - o **Problem**: Define a function that calculates the factorial of a number using a loop and returns the result.
   - o **Skills Practiced**: Looping inside functions, handling inputs, and return values.

5. **Password Validator Function**:
   - o **Problem**: Create a function that checks if a password meets certain criteria (e.g., length, uppercase letter, special character). Return True if valid, False otherwise.
   - o **Skills Practiced**: Conditional logic, return values, and function modularity.

6. **BMI Calculator with Functions**:
   - o **Problem**: Write a function that calculates Body Mass Index (BMI) given weight and height, and returns the BMI value along with a message indicating the BMI category.
   - o **Skills Practiced**: Parameter handling, return values, and applying logic within functions.

Expanded Practice Problems:

1. **Prime Number Checker**:
   - o **Problem**: Write a function that checks if a given number is prime and returns True or False.
   - o **Skills Practiced**: Using loops, conditionals, and return statements.

2. **Quadratic Equation Solver**:
   - o **Problem**: Define a function that solves quadratic equations using the quadratic formula, taking coefficients as parameters and returning solutions.
   - o **Skills Practiced**: Parameter handling, return values, and handling multiple outputs.

3. **User Menu with Functions**:
   - o **Problem**: Create a simple program with functions for common actions (e.g., displaying a menu,

checking balance, depositing money, withdrawing money) and a main function that calls them based on user input.

  o **Skills Practiced**: Modularity, return values, and using functions to organize larger programs.

4. **Circle Area and Circumference Calculator**:

  o **Problem**: Write two functions: one that calculates the area of a circle given its radius and one that calculates its circumference.

  o **Skills Practiced**: Parameter handling, return values, and using mathematical operations inside functions.

5. **Password Generator**:

  o **Problem**: Define a function that generates a random password of a specified length, using letters, numbers, and symbols.

  o **Skills Practiced**: Random number generation, function parameters, and string manipulation.

Mini Project: Expense Tracker

Objective: Create a program to track daily expenses, categorizing each expense (e.g., groceries, entertainment) and calculating daily totals. This project will reinforce modularity by breaking down the program into functions.

- **Problem Breakdown**:

o **Function 1**: Add a new expense entry with the date, category, and amount.

o **Function 2**: Display all expenses.

o **Function 3**: Calculate total expenses for a given day.

o **Function 4**: Calculate total expenses by category.

o **Main Function**: Control the flow of the program, allowing the user to choose actions.

o **Skills Practiced**: Parameter handling, using return values, organizing code with functions, and user interaction.

By the end of this chapter, readers will understand how to define and use functions to build modular and reusable code. They'll also gain insights into managing parameters, return values, and variable scope, setting a solid foundation for more advanced programming techniques.

CHAPTER 7: WORKING WITH LISTS

Lists are one of the most versatile data structures in Python, allowing you to store and manipulate collections of items. In this chapter, we'll cover how to create, access, and modify lists, explore common list methods, and work through practical examples.

Key Topics Covered:

1. **Introduction to Lists**
   - **Definition and Purpose**: Explanation of lists as ordered, mutable collections that can hold any type of data.
   - **Basic Syntax**: Creating a list with square brackets [] and understanding the concept of elements.
   - **Examples of Lists**: Lists of numbers, strings, mixed data types, and even lists within lists.

2. **Accessing List Elements**
   - **Indexing**: Accessing individual elements in a list using their index (e.g., my_list[0]).
   - **Negative Indexing**: Using negative indexes to access elements from the end of the list.
   - **Slicing**: Extracting a sublist by specifying a range of indexes (e.g., my_list[1:4]).
   - **Real-World Example**: Using a list to store temperatures for each day of the week and retrieving specific days or ranges.

3. **Modifying Lists**

- o **Changing Elements**: Assigning a new value to a specific index (e.g., my_list[2] = new_value).
- o **Adding Elements**: Appending elements to the end of the list with append() and inserting at a specific index with insert().
- o **Removing Elements**: Removing elements by value with remove(), by index with pop(), and using del.
- o **Real-World Example**: Managing a to-do list by adding, updating, and removing tasks.

4. **Common List Methods**
- o **append()**: Adding an item to the end of the list.
- o **insert()**: Inserting an item at a specified index.
- o **remove()**: Removing the first occurrence of a specified value.
- o **pop()**: Removing an item by index and returning it (commonly used for stack operations).
- o **index()**: Finding the index of the first occurrence of a value.
- o **count()**: Counting the occurrences of a specific value.
- o **sort() and sorted()**: Sorting the list in ascending or descending order.
- o **reverse()**: Reversing the order of items in the list.

- o **Real-World Example**: Organizing a list of students' scores by using sorting, finding the highest score, and counting specific grades.

5. **Iterating Over Lists**

   - o **Using for Loops**: Iterating over each element in a list using a for loop.
   - o **Using while Loops**: Iterating with a while loop when more control over the iteration is needed.
   - o **Enumerating Lists**: Using enumerate() to get both the index and value during iteration.
   - o **Real-World Example**: Calculating the average of a list of numbers by iterating through them.

6. **List Comprehensions**

   - o **Introduction to List Comprehensions**: Using list comprehensions to create lists in a concise way.
   - o **Basic Syntax**: Explanation of the syntax [expression for item in iterable if condition].
   - o **Examples**: Creating a list of squared numbers, filtering out even numbers, and transforming strings to uppercase.
   - o **Real-World Example**: Using list comprehensions to extract specific items from a list of dictionaries, like finding students who scored above a certain threshold.

Real-World Examples and Projects

1. **Shopping List Organizer**:
   - o **Problem**: Write a program that allows users to create a shopping list, add items, and remove items. Sort the list alphabetically and display the current list after each update.
   - o **Skills Practiced**: List manipulation, sorting, and list methods like append(), remove(), and sort().

2. **Grade Tracker**:
   - o **Problem**: Create a list to store scores from multiple students. Add scores, calculate the average, find the maximum score, and count how many students scored above a specific threshold.
   - o **Skills Practiced**: Using list methods like append(), count(), and iterating with loops.

3. **Inventory Management System**:
   - o **Problem**: Develop a simple inventory system where users can add items with quantities to an inventory list, update quantities, and remove items when they're out of stock.
   - o **Skills Practiced**: Managing lists of lists or dictionaries, list manipulation, and conditional logic.

4. **Employee Task Assignment**:
   - o **Problem**: Store a list of employees, assign tasks randomly, and keep track of completed tasks.

Display the updated task list after each task completion.

- o **Skills Practiced**: List indexing, updating list elements, and using random selections.

5. **To-Do List with Priority**:
    - o **Problem**: Create a to-do list where each task has a priority level. Sort the list by priority before displaying it, so high-priority tasks appear first.
    - o **Skills Practiced**: List sorting, append(), insert(), and handling lists of tuples.

Expanded Practice Problems

1. **Find Common Elements**:
    - o **Problem**: Write a function that takes two lists and returns a new list containing elements that appear in both lists.
    - o **Skills Practiced**: Iterating over lists, conditional logic, and using list comprehensions.

2. **Unique Elements Filter**:
    - o **Problem**: Given a list with duplicate values, return a new list containing only unique values.
    - o **Skills Practiced**: Using for loops, in keyword, and list comprehensions.

3. **Temperature Converter with Lists**:
   - ○ **Problem**: Ask the user for a list of temperatures in Celsius and convert each to Fahrenheit, storing the results in a new list.
   - ○ **Skills Practiced**: Iterating over lists, arithmetic, and list comprehensions.

4. **Survey Response Aggregator**:
   - ○ **Problem**: Store survey responses in a list. Calculate how many times each response was chosen and display the results.
   - ○ **Skills Practiced**: Using count(), iterating with for loops, and managing data in lists.

5. **Movie Title Filter**:
   - ○ **Problem**: Given a list of movie titles, create a new list containing only titles that start with a specific letter.
   - ○ **Skills Practiced**: List comprehensions, string manipulation, and filtering lists.

Mini Project: Simple Contact List

Objective: Build a simple contact list program that allows users to store and manage contacts, where each contact includes a name, phone number, and email. This project introduces the concept of lists within lists or lists of dictionaries.

- **Problem Breakdown**:
  - o **Add Contact**: Write a function that takes a name, phone number, and email, then adds them as a new entry in the contact list.
  - o **Remove Contact**: Allow users to delete a contact by name.
  - o **Search Contact**: Find and display contact information by searching for a name.
  - o **Display All Contacts**: Display all contacts, organized alphabetically by name.
  - o **Skills Practiced**: Using lists of dictionaries, iterating with for loops, and sorting lists.

By the end of this chapter, readers will be proficient with Python lists, able to use list methods, access and modify list elements, and create efficient and readable code using list comprehensions. With these skills, they'll be ready to handle larger data sets and more complex data manipulations in Python.

CHAPTER 8: DICTIONARIES AND SETS

Dictionaries and sets are powerful data structures in Python that allow you to handle data in unique ways. Dictionaries are ideal for creating key-value mappings, while sets are useful for storing unique values and performing efficient operations like unions and intersections. This chapter will provide a comprehensive overview of these structures, their practical applications, and how they can simplify your coding tasks.

Key Topics Covered

Part 1: Dictionaries

1. **Introduction to Dictionaries**
   - **Definition and Purpose**: Explanation of dictionaries as collections of key-value pairs, where each key is unique and used to access its corresponding value.
   - **Basic Syntax**: Creating a dictionary using curly braces {} with key-value pairs separated by colons, e.g., {"name": "Alice", "age": 25}.

- o **Example**: Using a dictionary to store information about a student, such as their name, age, and grade.

2. **Accessing and Modifying Dictionary Elements**
    - o **Accessing Values by Key**: Using bracket notation to retrieve a value by its key, e.g., student["name"].
    - o **Adding New Key-Value Pairs**: Assigning a value to a new key, e.g., student["major"] = "Math".
    - o **Modifying Existing Values**: Updating values by reassigning keys.
    - o **Removing Elements**: Using pop() to remove a specific key-value pair, del to delete a key, and clear() to empty the dictionary.
    - o **Real-World Example**: Using a dictionary to store user profile information and allowing updates.

3. **Common Dictionary Methods**
    - o **keys()**: Returns a list-like view of all the keys.
    - o **values()**: Returns a list-like view of all the values.
    - o **items()**: Returns a list of tuples, where each tuple is a key-value pair.
    - o **get()**: Safely accessing a value without raising a KeyError if the key doesn't exist.
    - o **update()**: Merging another dictionary or set of key-value pairs into the dictionary.

- o **Real-World Example**: A dictionary-based menu where each item name is the key, and its price is the value. Using update() to modify prices in bulk.

4. **Looping Through Dictionaries**
   - o **Looping Over Keys**: Using a for loop to iterate over keys.
   - o **Looping Over Values**: Iterating over values directly.
   - o **Looping Over Key-Value Pairs**: Using items() to loop over both keys and values simultaneously.
   - o **Real-World Example**: Displaying each item in a shopping cart along with its price by looping through a dictionary.

5. **Nested Dictionaries**
   - o **Creating Nested Structures**: Storing dictionaries within dictionaries to handle complex data structures, like a database of users where each user has personal information stored as key-value pairs.
   - o **Accessing Nested Data**: Using multiple levels of keys to retrieve deeply nested values.
   - o **Real-World Example**: A dictionary storing employee details, where each employee ID points to a nested dictionary of attributes (e.g., department, role, and salary).

Part 2: Sets

1. **Introduction to Sets**
   - **Definition and Purpose**: Explanation of sets as unordered collections of unique values, used to eliminate duplicates and perform mathematical set operations.
   - **Basic Syntax**: Creating a set with curly braces, e.g., {1, 2, 3}, or by using set() for an empty set.
   - **Example**: Using a set to store unique items in a list of purchases, ensuring no duplicates.

2. **Common Set Methods**
   - **Adding and Removing Elements**: Using add() to insert elements, remove() and discard() to delete elements (with discard() not raising an error if the element is absent).
   - **Set Operations**:
     - **Union** (| or union()): Combines elements from two sets.
     - **Intersection** (& or intersection()): Finds common elements between sets.
     - **Difference** (- or difference()): Elements present in one set but not in the other.
     - **Symmetric Difference** (^ or symmetric_difference()): Elements in either set but not both.

- o **Real-World Example**: Using sets to identify common customers between two different product lines.

3. **Looping Through Sets**

   - o **Using for Loops**: Iterating over a set's elements with a simple for loop.

   - o **Example**: Displaying each unique item in a list of purchases by first converting the list to a set.

4. **Set Comprehensions**

   - o **Definition and Syntax**: Using set comprehensions to create new sets with conditions and transformations.

   - o **Example**: Creating a set of unique words from a list of strings, filtering out short words.

Real-World Examples and Projects

1. **Product Inventory System with Dictionaries**

   - o **Problem**: Use a dictionary to track product quantities in inventory. Each product name is a key, and its quantity is the value. Implement options to add, update, or remove products and quantities.

   - o **Skills Practiced**: Dictionary creation, updating values, and looping through key-value pairs.

2. **Student Grades Tracker with Nested Dictionaries**
    - **Problem**: Store multiple students' grades for different subjects using a nested dictionary where each student has a dictionary of subjects and scores.
    - **Skills Practiced**: Nested dictionaries, updating nested values, and using loops for summary statistics.

3. **Unique Usernames with Sets**
    - **Problem**: Write a program that takes a list of usernames (some may be duplicates) and stores only the unique ones using a set. Allow users to check if a username is available.
    - **Skills Practiced**: Using sets to remove duplicates, set membership testing.

4. **Shared and Unique Customers with Sets**
    - **Problem**: Given two sets of customer IDs from two product lines, find customers who bought both products, only one, or neither.
    - **Skills Practiced**: Set operations (intersection, union, difference).

5. **Survey Results Aggregator with Dictionaries and Sets**
    - **Problem**: Track survey results where each response is stored as a dictionary entry with unique IDs. Use sets to keep track of unique respondents.

o **Skills Practiced**: Dictionary manipulation, using sets for uniqueness, and iterating over key-value pairs.

Expanded Practice Problems

1. **Menu Item Finder with Dictionaries**
   o **Problem**: Create a dictionary representing a restaurant menu with items as keys and prices as values. Write a function to search for an item and return its price.
   o **Skills Practiced**: Dictionary creation, accessing values by key, and handling missing keys with get().

2. **Library Book Tracker with Sets**
   o **Problem**: Track a library's collection of books using a set. Allow users to add, remove, or check the availability of books.
   o **Skills Practiced**: Set operations, adding and removing elements, and membership testing.

3. **Contact List Organizer with Nested Dictionaries**
   o **Problem**: Store contact details where each contact has a name, phone number, and email address as values in a nested dictionary.
   o **Skills Practiced**: Creating and accessing nested dictionaries.

4. **Common Words Finder with Sets**

o **Problem**: Given two lists of words (e.g., from two articles), create sets from each and find words that appear in both articles.

o **Skills Practiced**: Set operations (intersection), list-to-set conversion, and filtering duplicates.

5. **Word Frequency Counter with Dictionaries**

o **Problem**: Write a program that takes a paragraph of text, splits it into words, and counts the occurrences of each word using a dictionary.

o **Skills Practiced**: String manipulation, dictionary usage, and looping.

Mini Project: School Management System

Objective: Create a system for managing students, classes, and grades using dictionaries and sets.

- **Features**:

  o **Add Student**: Create a dictionary entry for each student with attributes like ID, name, and enrolled classes (stored as a set).

  o **Add Class**: Add new classes to each student's set of classes.

  o **Record Grades**: Store grades for each student in a nested dictionary.

  o **Display Summary**: Show a summary of each student's classes and grades.

○ **Skills Practiced**: Nested dictionaries, set operations, and dictionary manipulation.

By the end of this chapter, readers will have a strong understanding of dictionaries and sets, enabling them to handle unique data collections and create structured mappings. With these tools, they'll be prepared to build complex data structures and perform efficient operations for real-world applications.

CHAPTER 9: HANDLING STRINGS

Strings are a foundational data type in Python, essential for managing text in various applications. This chapter covers key string manipulation techniques, formatting methods, and practical exercises to build proficiency in handling text data effectively.

Key Topics Covered

1. **Introduction to Strings**
    - **Definition and Basic Syntax**: Understanding strings as sequences of characters, created by enclosing text in single (' ') or double (" ") quotes.
    - **Escaping Characters**: Using the backslash (\) to include special characters in strings, like quotes inside quotes (e.g., "He said, \"Hello!\"").
    - **Multiline Strings**: Using triple quotes (''' ''' or """ """) for strings that span multiple lines.
2. **Basic String Operations**

- o **Concatenation**: Joining strings using the + operator (e.g., "Hello, " + "world!").
- o **Repetition**: Repeating strings using the * operator (e.g., "ha" * 3).
- o **Length of a String**: Using len() to get the number of characters in a string.
- o **Real-World Example**: Building a user greeting message by concatenating the user's name and title.

3. **String Indexing and Slicing**

- o **Indexing**: Accessing individual characters using indexes (e.g., text[0] for the first character).
- o **Negative Indexing**: Using negative indexes to access characters from the end of the string.
- o **Slicing**: Extracting substrings by specifying a range of indexes (e.g., text[1:5]).
- o **Real-World Example**: Extracting parts of a URL (e.g., domain name) from a full web address using slicing.

4. **Common String Methods**

- o **Changing Case**: Converting strings to uppercase (upper()), lowercase (lower()), title case (title()), or capitalizing the first letter (capitalize()).
- o **Finding Substrings**: Using find() and index() to locate a substring within a string, and handling cases where the substring is absent.

- o **Replacing Text**: Using replace() to substitute one substring with another.
- o **Stripping Whitespace**: Removing unwanted spaces with strip(), lstrip(), and rstrip().
- o **Checking Content**: Using startswith(), endswith(), and isalpha() for specific checks on the content.
- o **Real-World Example**: Creating a formatted contact list by standardizing names (capitalizing) and stripping extra spaces.

5. **String Formatting**

- o **Old-Style Formatting**: Using % for formatting strings (e.g., "Hello, %s!" % name).
- o **str.format() Method**: Inserting values into placeholders with str.format(), and using positional and named placeholders (e.g., "Hello, {name}".format(name="Alice")).
- o **f-Strings (Formatted String Literals)**: Using f-strings (e.g., f"Hello, {name}!") for efficient and readable formatting.
- o **Precision Control**: Formatting numbers with specified decimal places (e.g., f"{value:.2f}").
- o **Alignment**: Adjusting text alignment within a formatted string using <, >, or ^ symbols in f-strings or format() for alignment.

- o **Real-World Example**: Formatting a report summary with aligned data fields, such as names, prices, and quantities.

6. **Advanced String Manipulation Techniques**
   - o **Splitting Strings**: Using split() to divide a string into a list based on a delimiter (e.g., spaces or commas).
   - o **Joining Strings**: Using join() to merge a list of strings into a single string with a specified separator.
   - o **Checking Substrings**: Using in and not in to test if a substring exists within a string.
   - o **Real-World Example**: Parsing CSV-formatted data by splitting lines into fields.

Real-World Examples and Projects

1. **Username Validator**
   - o **Problem**: Write a program that takes a username input and validates it, ensuring it contains only letters, numbers, or underscores, starts with a letter, and is between 5 and 15 characters.
   - o **Skills Practiced**: String indexing, isalpha(), isdigit(), and combining validation checks.

2. **Simple Text Formatter**

    o **Problem**: Create a function that takes a sentence, capitalizes the first letter of each word, and removes any extra spaces at the beginning and end.

    o **Skills Practiced**: String manipulation with strip() and title().

3. **Email Extractor**

    o **Problem**: Write a program that takes a block of text, searches for email addresses using find() or regular expressions, and extracts them into a list.

    o **Skills Practiced**: String searching, slicing, and list creation.

4. **Secure Password Generator**

    o **Problem**: Create a password generator function that generates a random password with uppercase, lowercase, digits, and special characters. Enforce a minimum length.

    o **Skills Practiced**: String concatenation, repetition, and join() for assembling characters.

5. **Sentence Analyzer**

    o **Problem**: Write a program that takes a sentence from the user and counts the number of words, characters, and unique letters.

    o **Skills Practiced**: Using split(), len(), and sets for unique values.

Expanded Practice Problems

1. **Palindrome Checker**
   - o **Problem**: Ask the user for a word, then check if it reads the same backward by reversing the string.
   - o **Skills Practiced**: Slicing for string reversal, lower() for case insensitivity.

2. **Text Replacement Program**
   - o **Problem**: Write a program that takes a paragraph of text and allows the user to replace specific words with others.
   - o **Skills Practiced**: Using replace() and handling dynamic user input.

3. **CSV Parser**
   - o **Problem**: Simulate reading a line from a CSV file and splitting it into individual fields.
   - o **Skills Practiced**: Using split() and join() to parse and reformat data.

4. **Hashtag Extractor**
   - o **Problem**: Given a sentence, extract words starting with # to identify hashtags.
   - o **Skills Practiced**: String indexing, startswith(), and splitting/joining.

5. **Initials Generator**
   - o **Problem**: Write a function that takes a full name as input and returns the initials.

o **Skills Practiced**: split() for names, list comprehension, and string concatenation.

Mini Project: Text-Based Report Generator

Objective: Build a program that generates a simple text-based report, summarizing data in a visually organized format.

- **Problem Breakdown**:
    - o **Input**: Allow users to enter data (e.g., names, departments, and scores).
    - o **Formatting**: Format the data into a report structure, with aligned columns and headers.
    - o **Output**: Print or save the report to a file.
    - o **Skills Practiced**: String formatting (f-strings), alignment, and using join() for clean data presentation.

By the end of this chapter, readers will be equipped to handle a wide range of text manipulation tasks in Python. They'll understand string basics, formatting, and advanced operations, preparing them for more complex projects that rely heavily on text data.

CHAPTER 10: FILE HANDLING

File handling is a vital skill for working with external data sources and saving data persistently. In this chapter, we'll cover how to read from and write to files, manage data in different file formats, and explore real-world examples of file processing.

Key Topics Covered

1. **Introduction to File Handling**
   o **File I/O Basics**: Understanding files as external data stores that can be read or written to from Python programs.
   o **Importance of File Handling**: Applications such as saving program data, loading configuration files, and processing external data.
2. **Opening and Closing Files**
   o **Opening Files**: Using the open() function to access files in different modes ('r' for read, 'w' for write, 'a' for append, 'r+' for read and write).

- o **Closing Files**: The importance of closing files after use to free system resources, using the close() method.
- o **Context Manager with with Statement**: Using with open(...) as f to automatically close files after use, ensuring resources are released even if an error occurs.
- o **Example**: Opening a text file to read content and then closing it manually and with with.

3. **Reading Files**
   - o **read() Method**: Reading the entire file content as a single string.
   - o **readline() and readlines() Methods**: Reading files line by line and reading all lines into a list.
   - o **Looping Over File Objects**: Using a for loop to read files line by line without loading the entire file into memory.
   - o **Real-World Example**: Reading a log file and printing each line to the console.

4. **Writing to Files**
   - o **write() Method**: Writing a single string to a file, which can overwrite existing content when used in write mode ('w').
   - o **writelines() Method**: Writing a list of strings to a file, commonly used for structured content.

- o **Appending to Files**: Using append mode ('a') to add new content to the end of a file without overwriting.
- o **Real-World Example**: Logging user activity by appending each action to a log file.

5. **File Paths and Directories**

- o **Absolute vs. Relative Paths**: Understanding the difference and when to use each.
- o **Creating Directories**: Using os.mkdir() to create directories and os.path to manage file paths.
- o **Real-World Example**: Saving files in a specific directory and using relative paths for easy file organization.

6. **Handling Different File Formats**

- o **Text Files (.txt)**: Handling simple text files for storing unstructured data.
- o **CSV Files**: Reading from and writing to CSV files using Python's built-in csv module, with examples of data processing.
- o **JSON Files**: Working with JSON files for structured data storage using Python's json module.
- o **Real-World Example**: Reading a CSV file containing user data, processing it, and saving updated data in JSON format.

7. **Error Handling in File Operations**

- **Common File Errors**: Handling common errors, such as FileNotFoundError and PermissionError.

- **Using Try-Except Blocks**: Wrapping file operations in try-except blocks to provide user-friendly error messages.

- **Real-World Example**: Attempting to open a user-specified file and catching errors if the file doesn't exist.

Real-World Examples and Projects

1. **Basic Contact Book**

   - **Problem**: Create a program to save, retrieve, and update contacts. Store each contact as a new line in a text file, with fields separated by commas.

   - **Skills Practiced**: Writing and reading text files, parsing line data, and handling user input.

2. **Log File Analyzer**

   - **Problem**: Write a program that reads a log file line by line, counting occurrences of keywords (e.g., "ERROR" or "WARNING") and printing a summary report.

   - **Skills Practiced**: Reading files, looping over lines, string searching, and summarizing data.

3. **CSV Data Processor**

   o **Problem**: Create a program that reads data from a CSV file, processes it (e.g., calculates averages or filters rows), and writes the results to a new CSV file.

   o **Skills Practiced**: Using the csv module, reading/writing rows, data manipulation.

4. **JSON Configuration Loader**

   o **Problem**: Build a program that reads a configuration file in JSON format, applies the settings, and allows users to save new settings back to the file.

   o **Skills Practiced**: Using the json module, working with dictionaries, file reading/writing, and handling JSON formatting.

5. **Survey Result Aggregator**

   o **Problem**: Write a program that reads survey results stored in a text file, aggregates the results by category, and writes a summary to a new file.

   o **Skills Practiced**: Reading and writing text files, string manipulation, and basic data processing.

Expanded Practice Problems

1. **Word Counter**
   - o **Problem**: Write a program that reads a text file, counts the occurrences of each word, and writes the results to a new file.
   - o **Skills Practiced**: Reading files, dictionaries for counting, writing output files.

2. **Data Backup Utility**
   - o **Problem**: Create a utility that copies a specified file to a backup directory, creating the directory if it doesn't exist.
   - o **Skills Practiced**: Using os for directory management, reading/writing files, and file paths.

3. **Temperature Data Logger**
   - o **Problem**: Develop a program that periodically writes temperature readings (simulated as random numbers) to a log file. Each entry should include the timestamp.
   - o **Skills Practiced**: File appending, timestamp generation, and data logging.

4. **Todo List Manager**
   - o **Problem**: Build a to-do list program that saves tasks to a text file. The program should allow users to add, delete, and view tasks.
   - o **Skills Practiced**: Writing/appending files, reading lists, and user interaction.

5. **URL Scraper and Saver**
   - o **Problem**: Create a program that reads URLs from a text file, fetches data from each URL (using the requests library), and saves the data to individual text files.
   - o **Skills Practiced**: Reading files, external library usage (e.g., requests), and saving data to files.

Mini Project: Expense Tracker

Objective: Build a simple expense tracker that saves each expense entry in a CSV file and allows users to view, add, and delete entries.

- **Problem Breakdown**:
  - o **Add Expense**: Prompt the user for an expense name, amount, and date, then save it to a CSV file.
  - o **View Expenses**: Read the CSV file and display all expenses, along with a running total.
  - o **Delete Expense**: Allow the user to delete an expense by name or date, updating the file.
  - o **Skills Practiced**: Using the csv module, reading and writing CSV files, data management.

This chapter covers essential file handling skills, equipping readers to work with text, CSV, and JSON files in various real-world scenarios. They'll understand how to read, write, and manage file data effectively, preparing them for data persistence and external data processing.

CHAPTER 11: ERROR HANDLING AND DEBUGGING

Error handling and debugging are crucial skills in programming that help ensure your code runs smoothly and is resilient to unexpected issues. In this chapter, we'll explore techniques for catching exceptions, using Python's built-in error handling tools, and effective debugging practices to make your code more robust and reliable.

Key Topics Covered

1. **Introduction to Errors and Exceptions**
   - **Syntax Errors vs. Exceptions**: Explanation of syntax errors (issues in code structure) and exceptions (runtime errors due to unexpected conditions).
   - **Common Exception Types**: Overview of frequently encountered exceptions:
     - ZeroDivisionError: Attempting to divide by zero.
     - ValueError: Incorrect value type for an operation.

- TypeError: Invalid operation between incompatible types.
- IndexError: Accessing a list index out of range.
- KeyError: Accessing a non-existent key in a dictionary.
  - **Real-World Example**: Demonstrating each exception with simple code snippets to highlight common pitfalls.

2. **Using try, except, and finally Blocks**
   - **Basic Syntax of try and except**: Wrapping code in try blocks to catch and handle exceptions, with except blocks to define specific actions based on error type.
   - **Handling Multiple Exceptions**: Using multiple except blocks to handle different exceptions and catch broader categories of errors.
   - **The finally Block**: Ensuring certain code always executes, regardless of whether an exception occurs (e.g., closing a file or releasing resources).
   - **Real-World Example**: Using try and except to handle user input errors, such as a non-numeric input when asking for a number.

3. **The else Block in Error Handling**

- o **Using else**: Executing code in the else block if no exceptions are raised in the try block.
- o **Example**: Calculating a result in a try block and printing a success message in else if no errors occurred.

4. **Raising Exceptions**

- o **raise Statement**: Manually raising exceptions when a specific condition is met, using custom error messages to communicate issues.
- o **Creating Custom Exceptions**: Defining custom exception classes to raise specialized errors relevant to your program.
- o **Real-World Example**: Creating a function to validate user input, raising an exception if the input is invalid.

5. **Debugging Techniques**

- o **Using print() Statements**: Basic debugging by inserting print() statements to track variable values and program flow.
- o **Debugging with Breakpoints**: Using breakpoints in an Integrated Development Environment (IDE) to pause program execution and inspect variables.
- o **The assert Statement**: Adding assertions to test assumptions in code and catch issues early, raising an AssertionError if a condition is False.

o **Real-World Example**: Debugging a function that calculates the area of a rectangle, with print statements to monitor intermediate steps and an assert statement to check for positive input values.

6. **Using Python's Built-In Debugger (pdb)**

   o **Introduction to pdb**: Overview of the Python Debugger (pdb) module and its common commands, such as step, next, continue, quit.

   o **Setting Breakpoints with pdb**: How to set breakpoints within the code and examine the state of variables.

   o **Real-World Example**: Debugging a function using pdb to inspect variable values at each step of execution.

7. **Logging Errors with the logging Module**

   o **Introduction to Logging**: Explanation of the logging module and its benefits over print() statements for error tracking.

   o **Basic Logging Levels**: Overview of logging levels (DEBUG, INFO, WARNING, ERROR, CRITICAL) and when to use each.

   o **Creating and Configuring Logs**: Setting up a log file and logging messages with different severity levels.

- o **Real-World Example**: Using logging to track errors and program flow in a data processing script, with logging.warning() for non-critical issues and logging.error() for major issues.

Real-World Examples and Projects

1. **Safe Division Function**
   - o **Problem**: Create a function that performs division, handling ZeroDivisionError by returning an error message instead of crashing.
   - o **Skills Practiced**: Using try and except, handling ZeroDivisionError, and returning meaningful feedback to users.

2. **User Input Validator**
   - o **Problem**: Write a function that asks for user input, handles ValueError if the input isn't a number, and raises a custom exception if the input is outside a valid range.
   - o **Skills Practiced**: Catching exceptions, raising custom exceptions, and validating input.

3. **File Reader with Error Handling**
   - o **Problem**: Create a program that opens and reads a file specified by the user. Use try-except to handle

FileNotFoundError if the file doesn't exist, and PermissionError if the program lacks permission to read the file.

- o **Skills Practiced**: File handling with error catching, handling multiple exceptions.

4. **Configuration File Loader with Logging**
   - o **Problem**: Write a program that loads configuration settings from a JSON file. Log an error if the file is missing or corrupted, and log warnings for any missing or deprecated configuration keys.
   - o **Skills Practiced**: Using logging for error tracking, try-except for handling file and JSON errors.

5. **Retrying Network Requests**
   - o **Problem**: Simulate a network request (e.g., API call) that retries multiple times upon failure, catching TimeoutError or ConnectionError and logging each retry attempt.
   - o **Skills Practiced**: Error handling, using loops with error-catching, and logging retry attempts.

Expanded Practice Problems

1. **Debugging a List Processing Function**

o **Problem**: Write a function that processes a list of numbers, catches TypeError if any item isn't a number, and uses print() debugging to track the flow of data.

o **Skills Practiced**: Using try-except, print() for debugging, and handling mixed data types.

2. **Simple Banking System with Error Handling**

o **Problem**: Create a mini banking program that allows deposits and withdrawals, raising an exception if the withdrawal amount exceeds the balance and logging errors when attempts fail.

o **Skills Practiced**: Custom exceptions, error logging, and input validation.

3. **API Response Validator**

o **Problem**: Write a function that validates data from an API response. Raise a ValueError if required fields are missing, and use logging to track successful validations and errors.

o **Skills Practiced**: Error handling with try-except, raise for custom validation, and logging.

4. **Database Connection Simulator with Debugging**

o **Problem**: Simulate a database connection attempt, catching ConnectionError if the connection fails, and using assert statements to verify that critical variables are set correctly.

  o **Skills Practiced**: Using assert, raising exceptions, and handling connection-related errors.

5. **E-Commerce Checkout System**

  o **Problem**: Write a program that processes orders and catches errors related to inventory shortages or invalid payment details. Use logging to track errors and debug output to verify inventory updates.

  o **Skills Practiced**: Error handling with custom exceptions, try-except for different error scenarios, and logging.

Mini Project: Student Grade Manager with Error Logging

Objective: Create a simple student grade manager program that reads from a file, calculates grades, and handles common errors (e.g., missing data, incorrect formats).

- **Problem Breakdown**:

  o **File Input**: Load student names and scores from a text file. Handle errors if the file is missing or incorrectly formatted.

  o **Grade Calculation**: Calculate the average score for each student, logging warnings if any scores are missing.

o **Error Logging**: Log errors for any missing data and provide feedback if calculations cannot proceed.

o **Skills Practiced**: File handling, error logging, custom error handling, and data validation.

By the end of this chapter, readers will be equipped with essential techniques for handling errors and debugging in Python. They'll know how to identify and catch exceptions, use debugging tools like print() and pdb, and leverage logging to monitor and track program behavior, preparing them to write more reliable and maintainable code.

CHAPTER 12: LIST COMPREHENSIONS AND GENERATOR EXPRESSIONS

List comprehensions and generator expressions are powerful tools in Python for creating lists and generating sequences efficiently. They provide a concise syntax for transforming and filtering data, and generator expressions allow memory-efficient operations, especially useful for large datasets. In this chapter, we'll explore both concepts, their syntax, and practical applications.

Key Topics Covered

1. **Introduction to List Comprehensions**
   - **Definition and Benefits**: Explanation of list comprehensions as a compact way to create lists by applying an expression to each item in an iterable.
   - **Basic Syntax**: Overview of the structure [expression for item in iterable if condition].
   - **Comparison to Traditional Loops**: Showing how list comprehensions can replace for loops for building lists, offering shorter and more readable code.

o **Example**: Generating a list of squares from 1 to 10 with a traditional loop vs. a list comprehension.

2. **Building Lists with List Comprehensions**
   o **Basic Examples**:
      ▪ Simple transformations, like creating a list of squares.
      ▪ Filtering with conditions, such as generating a list of even numbers.
   o **Real-World Example**: Creating a list of first names from a list of dictionary objects representing people.

3. **List Comprehensions with Conditional Logic**
   o **Single Condition**: Applying an if statement to include only specific items (e.g., numbers divisible by 3).
   o **If-Else Conditionals in List Comprehensions**: Using if and else within the comprehension for conditional expressions.
   o **Real-World Example**: Creating a list where numbers are squared if they're even and left as-is if they're odd.

4. **Nested List Comprehensions**
   o **Definition and Usage**: Using list comprehensions within list comprehensions for handling multi-dimensional data.
   o **Examples**:

- Flattening a list of lists.

- Creating a matrix with list comprehensions.

   o **Real-World Example**: Generating a 3x3 grid of coordinates (tuples) using nested list comprehensions.

5. **Dictionary and Set Comprehensions**

   o **Dictionary Comprehensions**: Similar syntax for dictionaries, {key: value for item in iterable if condition}.

- Example: Creating a dictionary where keys are numbers and values are their squares.

   o **Set Comprehensions**: Creating sets with unique values using {expression for item in iterable if condition}.

- Example: Extracting unique characters from a string.

   o **Real-World Example**: Using dictionary comprehensions to create a lookup table from a list of names and ages.

Part 2: Generator Expressions

1. **Introduction to Generator Expressions**

   o **Definition and Benefits**: Explanation of generator expressions as memory-efficient ways to generate sequences without storing the entire list in memory.

- o **Basic Syntax**: Overview of generator expression structure (expression for item in iterable if condition).
- o **Differences Between Generators and Lists**: Highlighting how generators are "lazy," generating items on demand, which conserves memory.
- o **Example**: Generating a sequence of squares for large ranges without storing the entire list.

2. **Using Generators in Practice**

- o **When to Use Generators**: Ideal scenarios for generators, such as when dealing with large datasets, infinite sequences, or data streams.
- o **Iterating Over Generators**: How to iterate over generators using for loops or next() to get items one by one.
- o **Real-World Example**: Reading a large log file line by line using a generator to avoid loading the entire file into memory.

3. **Combining Generators with Functions**

- o **Using yield in Functions**: Introduction to generator functions, using yield to produce items one at a time.
- o **Example**: Creating a generator function to yield Fibonacci numbers up to a certain limit.

o **Real-World Example**: A generator function that processes data from a sensor, yielding one data point at a time as it becomes available.

4. **Performance Comparison: List Comprehension vs. Generator Expression**

o **Memory Usage**: Comparing memory usage between list comprehensions and generator expressions when generating large sequences.

o **Execution Speed**: Understanding when list comprehensions may be faster due to direct list access, while generator expressions save memory.

o **Real-World Example**: Benchmarking a large sequence generation (e.g., a million numbers) with both techniques and observing memory consumption.

Real-World Examples and Projects

1. **Data Transformation with List Comprehensions**

o **Problem**: Write a program to transform a list of temperature readings from Celsius to Fahrenheit using list comprehension.

    o **Skills Practiced**: Basic transformation with list comprehension and applying a mathematical formula.

2. **Filtering Data with List Comprehensions**

    o **Problem**: Create a list of customers who have made purchases above a certain amount from a list of transaction data, using list comprehension.

    o **Skills Practiced**: Applying conditions in list comprehensions for filtering data.

3. **Flattening Nested Lists**

    o **Problem**: Given a list of lists representing daily transactions, flatten the list into a single list of transactions.

    o **Skills Practiced**: Nested list comprehensions and handling multi-dimensional data.

4. **Prime Numbers Generator**

    o **Problem**: Use a generator expression to create an infinite sequence of prime numbers, stopping after generating the first 100.

    o **Skills Practiced**: Generator expressions, conditional logic, and limiting a generator.

5. **File Processing with Generators**

    o **Problem**: Process a large text file line by line, filtering out lines containing a specific keyword using a generator.

o **Skills Practiced**: Generating sequences from file data and filtering large datasets without loading them into memory.

Expanded Practice Problems

1. **Word Length Filter with List Comprehension**
   o **Problem**: Write a program that takes a list of words and creates a new list with only words longer than five characters.
   o **Skills Practiced**: Filtering with list comprehension and handling strings.

2. **Character Frequency Counter**
   o **Problem**: Given a string, use a dictionary comprehension to count the frequency of each unique character.
   o **Skills Practiced**: Dictionary comprehension and string manipulation.

3. **File Line Counter with Generators**
   o **Problem**: Use a generator expression to count lines in a large file without loading it entirely into memory.
   o **Skills Practiced**: Using generator expressions to process files efficiently.

4. **Unique Words Extractor**
   - ○ **Problem**: Given a long paragraph, extract a set of unique words longer than four letters using set comprehension.
   - ○ **Skills Practiced**: Set comprehension, filtering, and handling text data.

5. **Batch Data Processor with Generators**
   - ○ **Problem**: Create a generator function that processes a large data list in batches of 100 items at a time, yielding each batch for further processing.
   - ○ **Skills Practiced**: Generator function design, yield, and handling large datasets.

Mini Project: Sales Data Filter and Summary

Objective: Create a program that reads a list of sales data (customer, amount) and uses comprehensions and generators to filter and summarize data.

- **Problem Breakdown**:
  - ○ **Data Filtering**: Use a list comprehension to filter sales above a certain threshold.
  - ○ **Data Summarization**: Use dictionary comprehension to summarize total sales per customer.

- ○ **Large Data Handling**: Use a generator expression to process each line of a large sales data file one at a time.
- ○ **Skills Practiced**: List, dictionary, and generator comprehensions for data processing and summarization.

By the end of this chapter, readers will be proficient with list comprehensions, dictionary and set comprehensions, and generator expressions. They'll know when and how to use these tools to write concise, efficient code, especially when handling large or complex data.

CHAPTER 13: WORKING WITH DATES AND TIMES

Python's datetime module is essential for handling date and time data, from logging activities to scheduling tasks. This chapter will cover the basics of the datetime module, key functions for working with dates and times, and practical examples for real-world applications.

Key Topics Covered

1. **Introduction to the datetime Module**
   - **Overview of datetime Components**: Explanation of the module's primary components:
     - **date**: Represents year, month, and day.
     - **time**: Represents hour, minute, second, and microsecond.

- **datetime**: Combines date and time into one class.
- **timedelta**: Represents differences between two dates or times.

o **Importing datetime**: Basic syntax for importing, such as from datetime import datetime, timedelta.

2. **Getting the Current Date and Time**

o **datetime.now()**: Retrieving the current date and time.

o **date.today()**: Getting today's date without the time component.

o **Example**: Displaying the current date and time in various formats.

3. **Creating and Formatting Dates and Times**

o **Creating Date and Time Objects**: Instantiating specific dates with date(year, month, day) and times with time(hour, minute, second).

o **String Formatting with strftime()**: Converting datetime objects to strings in various formats (e.g., "2023-11-13", "13/11/2023", "Monday, November 13").

o **Parsing Strings with strptime()**: Converting formatted strings into datetime objects.

o **Real-World Example**: Converting user input (like "2023-11-13") into a datetime object for validation.

4. **Calculations with Dates and Times**

   o   **Using timedelta**: Adding or subtracting days, hours, and minutes to/from datetime objects.

   o   **Finding Differences**: Calculating the difference between two dates/times to find durations in days, hours, or minutes.

   o   **Real-World Example**: Calculating the number of days until a user's birthday or upcoming event.

5. **Working with Time Zones**

   o   **Introduction to pytz Library**: Using the pytz library to work with time zones.

   o   **Setting and Converting Time Zones**: Assigning and converting time zones in datetime objects.

   o   **Example**: Scheduling meetings across different time zones and converting local times for attendees.

6. **Using Dates and Times in Applications**

   o   **Timestamping**: Adding timestamps to events for logging or tracking purposes.

   o   **Scheduling Tasks**: Example applications, such as checking if an event is overdue or setting reminders.

   o   **Real-World Example**: Implementing a simple task scheduler that triggers actions based on the current date and time.

7. **Date and Time Formatting for User-Friendly Output**

- o **Formatting Dates for Different Regions**: Adapting date formats for different user regions.

- o **Handling Relative Dates**: Converting dates to relative terms like "today," "yesterday," or "in 3 days" for improved readability.

- o **Real-World Example**: Displaying task due dates in a user-friendly format for a to-do list app.

Real-World Examples and Projects

1. **Event Countdown Timer**
   - o **Problem**: Write a program that takes a future date as input and calculates the days, hours, and minutes remaining until the event.
   - o **Skills Practiced**: Using timedelta, date arithmetic, and formatting for user-friendly output.

2. **Task Due Date Checker**
   - o **Problem**: Create a function that takes a list of task due dates and checks which tasks are overdue, due today, or due soon.
   - o **Skills Practiced**: Comparing dates, using timedelta for calculations, and filtering based on conditions.

3. **Time Zone Converter**

- o **Problem**: Build a time zone converter that allows users to input a time and convert it to a selected time zone.
- o **Skills Practiced**: Using the pytz library to assign and convert time zones, handling user input.

4. **Simple Stopwatch**

- o **Problem**: Implement a stopwatch program that starts timing when the user presses a button and stops when pressed again. Display the elapsed time.
- o **Skills Practiced**: Using datetime.now() to track time intervals, calculating time differences, and formatting elapsed time.

5. **Log File Timestamp Updater**

- o **Problem**: Write a program that reads a log file and appends timestamps to each log entry, indicating when it was processed.
- o **Skills Practiced**: Using datetime.now(), reading and writing to files, and formatting timestamps.

Expanded Practice Problems

1. **Age Calculator**

- o **Problem**: Create a program that asks the user for their birthdate and calculates their current age in years, months, and days.
- o **Skills Practiced**: Using date.today() and timedelta for calculating differences.

2. **Daily Reminder System**

- o **Problem**: Write a program that triggers a reminder at a specified time each day (e.g., 8:00 AM) and logs the reminder in a file.
- o **Skills Practiced**: Comparing times, scheduling daily tasks, and logging with timestamps.

3. **Monthly Calendar Generator**

- o **Problem**: Create a function that generates a calendar for a given month and year, displaying the days in a grid format.
- o **Skills Practiced**: Working with date, looping over days, and formatting output.

4. **Event Planner with Time Zones**

- o **Problem**: Develop an event planner that schedules events in multiple time zones and outputs the time for each participant based on their location.
- o **Skills Practiced**: Handling time zones, pytz library, and managing date conversions.

5. **Automatic Report Generator with Timestamps**

- o **Problem**: Create a program that generates a weekly report with the current timestamp and includes details like report generation time and duration.
- o **Skills Practiced**: Using datetime for generating timestamps, calculating report duration, and automating tasks.

Mini Project: To-Do List with Due Dates and Reminders

Objective: Build a to-do list program that tracks task due dates, reminds users of approaching deadlines, and marks overdue tasks.

- **Problem Breakdown**:
  - o **Add Task**: Allow users to add tasks with due dates.
  - o **Check Deadlines**: Regularly check tasks to see if they are overdue, due today, or due soon.
  - o **Display Tasks**: Format task list with due dates and status (e.g., "due today," "overdue").
  - o **Skills Practiced**: Using datetime for date calculations, formatting for user-friendly output, and scheduling reminders.

By the end of this chapter, readers will be proficient with Python's datetime module, enabling them to handle a wide range of date and time operations. They'll be able to create applications that schedule, log, and manage time-based data effectively, preparing them for projects that require accurate timing and scheduling.

CHAPTER 14: DATA ANALYSIS WITH PANDAS BASICS

Pandas is a powerful data manipulation library in Python that makes it easy to work with structured data, especially in tabular form. This chapter introduces the basics of the Pandas library, focusing on creating, manipulating, and analyzing data with DataFrames and Series. These skills form the foundation for more advanced data analysis tasks.

Key Topics Covered

1. **Introduction to Pandas**

o **Overview of Pandas**: Explanation of Pandas as a library for data manipulation, ideal for handling large datasets, transforming data, and performing statistical operations.

o **Installation and Setup**: Installing Pandas using pip install pandas, importing it with the alias pd, and setting up the coding environment.

2. **Data Structures in Pandas**

o **Series**: One-dimensional labeled arrays, often used for single columns of data.

- Creating a Series from lists and dictionaries.
- Accessing elements in a Series by index and label.

o **DataFrames**: Two-dimensional labeled data structures (like a table with rows and columns).

- Creating a DataFrame from dictionaries, lists of dictionaries, and CSV files.
- Accessing rows and columns using .loc[], .iloc[], and direct indexing.

o **Real-World Example**: Creating a DataFrame to represent sales data for different products.

3. **Loading and Saving Data**

o **Reading Data from CSV Files**: Using pd.read_csv() to load CSV data into a DataFrame.

- o **Writing Data to CSV Files**: Saving DataFrames to CSV files with to_csv().
- o **Reading and Writing Excel Files**: Using pd.read_excel() and to_excel() for Excel file handling (requires openpyxl or xlsxwriter libraries).
- o **Real-World Example**: Loading a dataset of customer orders from a CSV file and saving processed data to a new file.

4. **Basic DataFrame Operations**
   - o **Viewing Data**: Using .head(), .tail(), and .info() to get a quick summary of the DataFrame.
   - o **Inspecting Data Types**: Checking column data types with .dtypes and converting them with .astype().
   - o **Sorting Data**: Sorting rows with .sort_values(), by column values in ascending or descending order.
   - o **Filtering and Selecting Data**: Filtering rows based on conditions (e.g., df[df['sales'] > 1000]).
   - o **Real-World Example**: Sorting a dataset by sales and filtering to show only records where sales exceed a specific threshold.

5. **Exploring and Summarizing Data**
   - o **Descriptive Statistics**: Using .describe() to get summary statistics for numerical columns (mean, median, count, etc.).

- o **Aggregating Data**: Using .sum(), .mean(), .min(), .max(), and .count() for quick data aggregation.
- o **Grouping Data**: Grouping data by columns with .groupby() to calculate aggregate statistics, such as total sales per region.
- o **Real-World Example**: Analyzing monthly sales data to calculate total sales per product category.

6. **Handling Missing Data**
   - o **Identifying Missing Values**: Using .isnull() and .notnull() to locate missing values in the DataFrame.
   - o **Handling Missing Data**: Options for handling missing data, including .dropna() to remove rows with missing values and .fillna() to fill in missing values.
   - o **Real-World Example**: Replacing missing customer ages in a dataset with the median age and dropping rows with empty email addresses.

7. **Data Cleaning and Transformation**
   - o **Renaming Columns**: Renaming columns with .rename() for better readability and consistency.
   - o **Changing Column Types**: Converting data types using .astype() for numerical or categorical analysis.
   - o **Applying Functions to Columns**: Using .apply() to modify column values (e.g., converting all text to lowercase or calculating discounts).

o **Real-World Example**: Cleaning a dataset of product reviews by standardizing column names, converting dates, and removing unnecessary columns.

Real-World Examples and Projects

1. **Customer Segmentation Analysis**
   o **Problem**: Load a dataset of customer purchases, calculate the average purchase per customer, and segment customers into high, medium, and low spenders.
   o **Skills Practiced**: Loading data, grouping by customer ID, and applying conditional column creation.

2. **Sales Performance Report**
   o **Problem**: Write a program that loads monthly sales data, calculates the total sales per region, and outputs a summary report.
   o **Skills Practiced**: Aggregating data with groupby, using .sum() and .describe(), and saving to CSV.

3. **Product Inventory Checker**

- o **Problem**: Create a program that loads inventory data, checks stock levels, and filters for items that are below the reorder threshold.
- o **Skills Practiced**: Filtering rows based on conditions and basic arithmetic operations.

4. **Employee Attendance Tracker**
   - o **Problem**: Load employee attendance records, calculate total attendance days per employee, and identify any employee with attendance below a set threshold.
   - o **Skills Practiced**: Reading data, grouping and aggregating, and filtering results.

5. **Movie Ratings Analyzer**
   - o **Problem**: Load a dataset of movie ratings, calculate the average rating per genre, and sort movies by popularity.
   - o **Skills Practiced**: Grouping by genre, calculating averages, and sorting data.

Expanded Practice Problems

1. **Temperature Data Analysis**

o **Problem**: Load daily temperature readings, calculate the monthly average temperature, and identify the hottest day.

o **Skills Practiced**: Grouping by month, calculating averages, and using .idxmax().

2. **COVID-19 Case Tracker**

o **Problem**: Load a dataset of COVID-19 cases, group by country, and calculate the total cases and deaths per country.

o **Skills Practiced**: Grouping, summing columns, and sorting data.

3. **E-commerce Sales Summary**

o **Problem**: Analyze a dataset of e-commerce transactions to calculate total sales by product category and identify the top 5 best-selling products.

o **Skills Practiced**: Grouping, filtering, and sorting.

4. **Airline Data Analysis**

o **Problem**: Load a dataset of airline flight data, filter for delayed flights, and calculate average delay time per airline.

o **Skills Practiced**: Filtering, grouping, and calculating mean values.

5. **Restaurant Order Analysis**

- o **Problem**: Load a dataset of restaurant orders, group by menu item, and calculate total quantity sold and average sale price per item.
- o **Skills Practiced**: Aggregating data and calculating summary statistics.

Mini Project: Sales Data Dashboard

Objective: Build a simple sales data dashboard that provides insights into monthly and quarterly sales performance.

- **Problem Breakdown**:
  - o **Load Data**: Load a dataset of daily sales transactions, including date, product, and sales amount.
  - o **Calculate Monthly and Quarterly Totals**: Aggregate data by month and quarter to calculate total sales for each period.
  - o **Identify Top Products**: Group by product and calculate the total sales to identify the top 5 products.
  - o **Output Summary**: Print a summary table with total sales by period and top products.
  - o **Skills Practiced**: Data loading, grouping, aggregation, and data presentation.

By the end of this chapter, readers will be familiar with the basics of Pandas, including loading, cleaning, manipulating, and analyzing data. They'll be equipped to handle real-world data analysis tasks, creating the foundation needed for more advanced data science and machine learning projects.

CHAPTER 15: API INTEGRATION

APIs (Application Programming Interfaces) enable applications to communicate with external services to access data, trigger actions, or perform complex operations. In this chapter, we'll explore how to connect with APIs, make requests, and process JSON responses using Python, allowing you to enhance your applications with real-time data and powerful external functionality.

Key Topics Covered

1. **Introduction to APIs**

   o **What is an API?**: Overview of APIs as intermediaries between applications that enable data exchange and service access.

   o **Types of APIs**: REST (Representational State Transfer) APIs and their widespread use for web services, including other types like SOAP and GraphQL.

   o **Real-World Use Cases**: Common API applications, such as accessing weather data, social media integration, and working with payment gateways.

2. **Making API Requests with requests Library**

   o **Installing and Importing requests**: Basic setup, including installation (pip install requests).

   o **Making GET Requests**: Using requests.get() to retrieve data from APIs.

   o **Status Codes**: Understanding HTTP status codes (e.g., 200 OK, 404 Not Found, 500 Internal Server Error) and handling them in code.

   o **Real-World Example**: Making a GET request to an open weather API to retrieve current weather data.

3. **Understanding JSON Data**

- o **What is JSON?**: Explanation of JSON (JavaScript Object Notation) as a lightweight format for structuring data.
- o **JSON Structure**: Examples of JSON objects, arrays, and key-value pairs.
- o **Converting JSON Data**: Parsing JSON with .json() to convert the API response to a Python dictionary.
- o **Real-World Example**: Retrieving JSON data from an API and printing specific data, like a temperature reading from a weather response.

4. **Processing API Data**
- o **Accessing Nested Data**: Navigating through nested JSON structures to retrieve specific values.
- o **Error Handling**: Handling errors with try-except blocks when parsing JSON and managing invalid or unexpected data.
- o **Real-World Example**: Accessing data in a nested JSON response from a COVID-19 statistics API, displaying country-specific case counts.

5. **Sending Data with POST Requests**
- o **Making POST Requests**: Using requests.post() to send data to APIs.
- o **Sending JSON Data**: Formatting Python data as JSON using json.dumps() and sending it in the POST request payload.

    o **Real-World Example**: Posting a new blog entry or comment to a content management API, sending user data in JSON format.

6. **API Authentication and Authorization**

    o **Types of Authentication**: Overview of common authentication types, such as API keys, OAuth, and bearer tokens.

    o **Using API Keys**: Attaching API keys to requests in headers or query parameters for access control.

    o **Real-World Example**: Integrating with a secure API (e.g., Twitter or GitHub API) using an API key for authorization.

7. **Practical API Integration Examples**

    o **Weather App**: Building a simple application that retrieves and displays real-time weather data based on the user's location.

    o **Currency Converter**: Using an API to fetch live exchange rates and converting amounts between different currencies.

    o **Real-World Example**: Retrieving historical stock prices from a financial API and displaying trends over time.

Real-World Examples and Projects

1. **Weather Information Retriever**

   o **Problem**: Write a program that takes a city name as input, queries a weather API, and displays the current temperature, humidity, and weather conditions.

   o **Skills Practiced**: Making GET requests, parsing JSON data, and error handling.

2. **News Headlines Fetcher**

   o **Problem**: Connect to a news API, retrieve the latest headlines for a given category, and display the results in a clean format.

   o **Skills Practiced**: Making requests with parameters, working with JSON, and displaying structured data.

3. **Social Media Post Scheduler**

   o **Problem**: Create a program that schedules social media posts by connecting to an API (e.g., Twitter API) and posts at specified times.

   o **Skills Practiced**: Using POST requests, handling JSON data, and scheduling tasks.

4. **Crypto Price Tracker**

   o **Problem**: Retrieve live cryptocurrency prices from a crypto API and display changes in price over a specified period.

o **Skills Practiced**: Using GET requests, working with JSON data, and implementing a simple dashboard for price tracking.

5. **Flight Price Monitor**

o **Problem**: Create a tool that checks flight prices for specific routes and alerts the user if the price drops below a specified amount.

o **Skills Practiced**: Working with parameters in GET requests, handling JSON responses, and applying conditional logic for notifications.

Expanded Practice Problems

1. **COVID-19 Statistics by Country**

o **Problem**: Retrieve COVID-19 statistics by country from a public API and display data like total cases, recoveries, and deaths.

o **Skills Practiced**: Parsing nested JSON structures, handling API parameters, and formatting data for display.

2. **Stock Market Data Fetcher**

o **Problem**: Write a program that retrieves historical stock prices for a given company and calculates the average price over the past month.

o **Skills Practiced**: Parsing JSON data, handling date-based parameters, and calculating averages.

3. **Book Finder**

o **Problem**: Create a book search tool that connects to a book API (e.g., Google Books API), takes a search term, and displays matching book titles and authors.

o **Skills Practiced**: Using parameters in GET requests, parsing JSON, and handling errors for unrecognized search terms.

4. **Email Notification System**

o **Problem**: Integrate with an email API (like SendGrid) to create a notification system that sends automated emails based on specific triggers (e.g., new data from an API).

o **Skills Practiced**: Using POST requests, sending JSON data, and handling authentication.

5. **Geolocation and Mapping Tool**

o **Problem**: Use a geolocation API to determine the user's location based on IP and display a map of nearby landmarks or places of interest.

o **Skills Practiced**: API integration, working with coordinates, and handling geolocation data.

Mini Project: Real-Time Currency Converter

Objective: Build a real-time currency converter that retrieves current exchange rates from an API and converts between specified currencies.

- **Problem Breakdown**:
  - **Fetch Exchange Rates**: Use a currency API to fetch current exchange rates in real-time.
  - **User Input**: Allow the user to enter the amount and the source and target currencies.
  - **Calculate Conversion**: Convert the amount using the fetched exchange rate.
  - **Error Handling**: Handle cases where the API fails or the user enters invalid currency codes.
  - **Skills Practiced**: GET requests, parsing JSON data, user input validation, and error handling.

By the end of this chapter, readers will understand the basics of API integration, enabling them to connect with and leverage external services to enhance their applications. They'll be equipped to work with APIs that return JSON data, authenticate requests, and perform common API operations, forming a strong foundation for building data-driven applications.

CHAPTER 16: BASIC WEB SCRAPING

Web scraping is the process of extracting data from websites, enabling automation of data collection for various applications, such as tracking prices, gathering information, and monitoring trends. In this chapter, we'll explore basic web scraping techniques using Python's requests library and BeautifulSoup for parsing HTML content. We'll also discuss ethical considerations and best practices to ensure responsible scraping.

Key Topics Covered

1. **Introduction to Web Scraping**
   - o **Definition and Applications**: Explanation of web scraping and its common uses, such as price monitoring, data collection, and content aggregation.
   - o **Ethical Considerations**: Importance of ethical scraping, respecting a website's robots.txt file, and only scraping publicly available data. Emphasizing the need to avoid excessive requests that could burden a website's server.
   - o **Legal Concerns**: Brief overview of legal limitations, such as adhering to website terms of service, and understanding when scraping is permissible.

2. **Setting Up with requests and BeautifulSoup**
   - o **Installing Libraries**: Instructions for installing requests and BeautifulSoup using pip install requests beautifulsoup4.
   - o **Importing Modules**: Basic imports for scraping projects (requests for HTTP requests and bs4 for HTML parsing).
   - o **Making an HTTP Request**: Using requests.get() to fetch a webpage and checking the response status.
   - o **Real-World Example**: Making a request to a news website and retrieving the raw HTML content.

3. **Parsing HTML with BeautifulSoup**

- o **Creating a BeautifulSoup Object**: Loading HTML content into BeautifulSoup for parsing.

- o **Understanding HTML Structure**: Brief overview of HTML tags and attributes (e.g., <div>, <span>, <a>), and how to identify content of interest in a webpage.

- o **Basic HTML Parsing**: Using BeautifulSoup methods like .find(), .find_all(), and accessing tag attributes to extract data.

- o **Real-World Example**: Scraping headlines from a news site by targeting specific HTML tags and classes.

4. **Navigating and Extracting Data**

- o **Using CSS Selectors**: Finding elements with specific CSS classes or IDs using .select() and .select_one().

- o **Accessing Text and Attributes**: Retrieving text content with .text and accessing tag attributes (e.g., href for links).

- o **Real-World Example**: Extracting product names and prices from an e-commerce page using CSS selectors.

5. **Looping Through Multiple Elements**

- o **Finding All Elements of a Type**: Using .find_all() to select all elements of a certain tag or class.

- o **Looping Through Results**: Iterating through the results to collect and store data, such as all blog post titles on a website.
- o **Real-World Example**: Scraping job listings from a job board by looping through each listing on the page.

6. **Storing Scraped Data**

- o **Saving to CSV**: Using Python's csv module to save scraped data to a CSV file.
- o **Saving to JSON**: Using the json module to store structured data.
- o **Real-World Example**: Scraping book information (title, author, price) and saving it as a CSV file for analysis.

7. **Dealing with Pagination**

- o **Understanding Pagination**: How websites split content across multiple pages and how to identify pagination links.
- o **Navigating Multiple Pages**: Using loops to scrape data from multiple pages by updating the URL or using the next button.
- o **Real-World Example**: Scraping multiple pages of product listings from an e-commerce site.

8. **Handling Common Obstacles in Web Scraping**

- o **User-Agent Headers**: Setting custom headers to mimic a browser request and avoid blocking by websites.
- o **Delays and Throttling**: Adding delays with time.sleep() between requests to avoid overloading the server and minimize detection.
- o **Handling Errors**: Using try-except blocks to manage failed requests, missing elements, or invalid pages.
- o **Real-World Example**: Scraping stock prices from a financial website with custom headers and throttling requests.

Real-World Examples and Projects

1. **Weather Information Scraper**
   - o **Problem**: Write a program that retrieves the current temperature and weather conditions from a weather website for a specific location.
   - o **Skills Practiced**: Making requests, parsing HTML, and using CSS selectors to find weather data.
2. **Real Estate Listings Scraper**

    o **Problem**: Create a scraper that extracts information on available properties (e.g., price, location, number of bedrooms) from a real estate website.

    o **Skills Practiced**: Navigating HTML structures, using .find_all(), and storing data in a CSV file.

3. **E-commerce Price Tracker**

    o **Problem**: Build a tool that scrapes product prices from an e-commerce site and alerts the user when a price drops below a certain threshold.

    o **Skills Practiced**: Extracting product information, saving data for comparison, and setting up automated notifications.

4. **Job Listings Aggregator**

    o **Problem**: Scrape job titles, companies, and locations from a job board and save the data to a structured format.

    o **Skills Practiced**: Looping through elements, extracting multiple data points, and handling pagination.

5. **Social Media Hashtag Scraper**

    o **Problem**: Collect the latest posts or hashtags from a social media site's public pages to track trends or popularity.

o **Skills Practiced**: Using BeautifulSoup for parsing and data extraction, handling nested tags, and storing data for analysis.

Expanded Practice Problems

1. **Sports Scores Scraper**

   o **Problem**: Scrape scores and results from a sports website, filtering by a specific team or event.

   o **Skills Practiced**: Parsing structured data, working with nested tags, and saving data for further analysis.

2. **News Aggregator**

   o **Problem**: Write a scraper that gathers headlines and links from multiple news websites and aggregates them into a single file.

   o **Skills Practiced**: Using multiple requests, parsing different HTML structures, and saving data in a structured format.

3. **Amazon Product Review Scraper**

   o **Problem**: Scrape user reviews for a given product on Amazon, including the star rating and review text.

- o **Skills Practiced**: Parsing reviews, working with pagination, and managing large text data.

4. **Wikipedia Data Scraper**
   - o **Problem**: Extract structured information from a Wikipedia page (e.g., an infobox table) about a specific topic.
   - o **Skills Practiced**: Navigating complex HTML structures, parsing table data, and handling unique page layouts.

5. **Stock Market Data Extractor**
   - o **Problem**: Write a program to scrape real-time stock prices for selected companies, saving the results for later analysis.
   - o **Skills Practiced**: Handling dynamic pages, parsing numerical data, and setting up a timed scraping process.

Mini Project: Book Information Scraper

Objective: Build a web scraper that collects data on books from an online bookstore, including title, author, price, and rating, and saves it to a CSV file for analysis.

- **Problem Breakdown**:

- o **Target Data**: Extract book titles, authors, prices, and ratings.
- o **Pagination Handling**: Scrape data from multiple pages to collect a full list of books.
- o **Save to CSV**: Store the data in a CSV file for future analysis.
- o **Skills Practiced**: HTML parsing, CSS selectors, looping through pages, and handling structured data output.

By the end of this chapter, readers will understand the basics of web scraping, including using the requests library to retrieve data and BeautifulSoup to parse HTML. They'll be able to build basic scrapers that collect data responsibly and save it in structured formats for analysis, with a strong understanding of ethical and legal considerations.

CHAPTER 17: OBJECT-ORIENTED PROGRAMMING (OOP)

Object-Oriented Programming (OOP) is a powerful paradigm in Python that enables developers to create reusable, modular, and organized code through the use of classes and objects. In this chapter, we'll cover the fundamentals of OOP, including classes, objects, inheritance, encapsulation, and hands-on exercises to solidify these concepts.

Key Topics Covered

1. **Introduction to Object-Oriented Programming**
   o **What is OOP?**: Overview of OOP as a programming paradigm that organizes code around objects rather than functions and logic alone.
   o **Key OOP Principles**: Explanation of core principles like encapsulation, inheritance, abstraction, and polymorphism.
   o **Real-World Analogy**: Drawing parallels to real-world objects (e.g., a "Car" class with attributes like "color" and "model," and behaviors like "drive" and "stop").

2. **Defining Classes and Creating Objects**
   o **Classes**: Explanation of classes as blueprints for creating objects, with attributes (properties) and methods (functions).
   o **Creating a Class**: Syntax for defining a class with the class keyword, defining attributes, and creating a basic method.
   o **Creating Objects**: Instantiating an object from a class and accessing its attributes and methods.
   o **Example**: Defining a Car class with attributes like make and model, and methods like start() and stop().

3. **Attributes and Methods**

   o **Instance Attributes**: Using __init__() to initialize instance attributes and defining attributes unique to each object.

   o **Class Attributes**: Defining attributes that are shared across all instances of a class.

   o **Methods**: Defining methods within a class, including instance methods (which operate on specific objects) and static methods.

   o **Real-World Example**: Creating a Book class with instance attributes for title and author, a class attribute for publisher, and methods to check availability.

4. **Encapsulation and Data Hiding**

   o **Encapsulation**: Explanation of encapsulation as the practice of keeping data and methods private to prevent unwanted interference.

   o **Public vs. Private Attributes**: Using naming conventions (single underscore _ and double underscore __) to indicate private attributes and methods.

   o **Getter and Setter Methods**: Creating methods to get (retrieve) and set (modify) private attributes safely.

- o **Real-World Example**: Creating a BankAccount class where the balance is private and can only be accessed or modified through deposit() and withdraw() methods.

5. **Inheritance and Code Reusability**

   - o **Inheritance Basics**: Defining a subclass that inherits attributes and methods from a superclass, promoting code reusability.

   - o **Extending and Overriding Methods**: Adding new methods to subclasses and overriding inherited methods for customized behavior.

   - o **Using super()**: Calling the superclass's methods from a subclass to extend functionality.

   - o **Real-World Example**: Defining a Vehicle superclass with basic attributes and creating Car and Truck subclasses with additional methods specific to each type.

6. **Polymorphism and Method Overloading**

   - o **Polymorphism**: Explanation of polymorphism as the ability of different classes to provide different implementations for the same method.

   - o **Method Overloading in Python**: Using different methods with the same name (e.g., __str__() method in each subclass to print custom information).

- o **Duck Typing**: Leveraging Python's dynamic typing to write code that operates on any object that supports the expected behavior, regardless of class.
- o **Real-World Example**: Creating Dog and Cat classes that both implement a speak() method with unique outputs ("bark" vs. "meow").

7. **Practical Applications of OOP**

- o **Modeling Complex Systems**: Using OOP to represent complex systems with multiple entities and relationships (e.g., a school system with Student, Teacher, and Course classes).
- o **Code Reusability**: Creating libraries of reusable classes that can be used in multiple projects.
- o **Real-World Example**: Building a simple customer management system with Customer, Order, and Product classes.

Real-World Examples and Projects

1. **Bank Account Management System**

- o **Problem**: Create a BankAccount class with methods to deposit, withdraw, and display the current balance. Extend it to include a SavingsAccount subclass with interest calculation.
- o **Skills Practiced**: Encapsulation, inheritance, and using getters/setters.

2. **Library Management System**

   o **Problem**: Build a Library class with methods to add books, borrow books, and return books. Define a Book class with details like title, author, and availability.

   o **Skills Practiced**: Class composition, encapsulation, and data handling.

3. **Employee Management System**

   o **Problem**: Create an Employee class with basic information (name, position, salary) and methods to update salary and display details. Add a Manager subclass with additional attributes (e.g., team).

   o **Skills Practiced**: Inheritance, polymorphism, and method overriding.

4. **Shopping Cart System**

   o **Problem**: Implement a ShoppingCart class where users can add, remove, and view products. Define a Product class with attributes like name and price.

   o **Skills Practiced**: Composition (classes working together) and method chaining.

5. **Online Course Management System**

   o **Problem**: Define Course, Student, and Instructor classes to manage course enrollments, assignments, and grading.

o **Skills Practiced**: Creating relationships between classes, inheritance, and encapsulation.

Expanded Practice Problems

1. **Rental Car System**
   - o **Problem**: Write a program that models a rental car system. Define Car and RentalCar classes to manage car availability and rental records.
   - o **Skills Practiced**: Inheritance, class relationships, and encapsulation.

2. **Inventory Management System**
   - o **Problem**: Implement a Product class and Inventory class to track stock levels, add items, and remove items from inventory.
   - o **Skills Practiced**: Class composition and data encapsulation.

3. **Game Character System**
   - o **Problem**: Create a system for game characters with a base Character class and subclasses for specific character types (e.g., Warrior, Mage) with unique abilities.
   - o **Skills Practiced**: Inheritance, polymorphism, and method overloading.

4. **Zoo Management System**

   o **Problem**: Define classes for Animal, Mammal, Bird, and Reptile, each with different attributes and methods to track feeding and habitat needs.

   o **Skills Practiced**: Inheritance, polymorphism, and managing hierarchical class structures.

5. **Task Scheduler**

   o **Problem**: Implement a Task class with attributes like description, due date, and priority. Create a TaskScheduler class to manage and prioritize tasks.

   o **Skills Practiced**: Data encapsulation, class relationships, and basic data management.

Mini Project: E-commerce Platform with OOP

Objective: Build an e-commerce system using OOP principles. Create classes to represent Product, Customer, Order, and ShoppingCart.

- **Problem Breakdown**:

   o **Product Class**: Define attributes like name, price, and stock quantity.

   o **Customer Class**: Include customer details (name, email) and purchase history.

- ○ **ShoppingCart Class**: Add and remove products, calculate the total price, and apply discounts.
- ○ **Order Class**: Record order details, including customer info, purchased items, and the total amount.
- ○ **Skills Practiced**: Encapsulation, inheritance, relationships between classes, and creating a small system with interacting components.

By the end of this chapter, readers will have a solid understanding of OOP fundamentals in Python, including defining classes and objects, using inheritance and polymorphism, and applying encapsulation. They'll be able to design and implement modular systems with reusable components, preparing them for building complex, object-oriented applications.

CHAPTER 18: RECURSION AND BACKTRACKING

Recursion is a fundamental programming technique where a function calls itself to solve problems in a divide-and-conquer approach. Paired with backtracking, recursion can be highly effective for complex problems requiring exploration of multiple paths or solutions. This chapter delves into the mechanics of recursion, how it works, practical use cases, and an introduction to backtracking for solving more advanced problems.

Key Topics Covered

1. **Introduction to Recursion**
   o **What is Recursion?**: Explanation of recursion as a process where a function calls itself to solve smaller instances of the same problem.
   o **Base Case and Recursive Case**: Explanation of the need for a base case to stop recursion and a recursive case to break down the problem.
   o **Call Stack and Memory Usage**: Understanding the call stack, how recursive calls accumulate, and why excessive recursion can lead to stack overflow errors.
   o **Real-World Example**: Illustrating recursion with a simple countdown function that calls itself with a decreasing number until it reaches zero.

2. **Simple Recursive Problems**
   o **Factorial Calculation**: Writing a recursive function to calculate the factorial of a number, highlighting base and recursive cases.

- o **Fibonacci Sequence**: Implementing a recursive function to compute Fibonacci numbers, showcasing how recursive calls create a tree structure.

- o **Sum of a List**: Writing a recursive function to calculate the sum of elements in a list, dividing the list into smaller parts until reaching a single element.

- o **Real-World Example**: Using recursion to navigate hierarchical file systems (folder structures) by traversing subfolders and files.

3. **Analyzing Recursive Algorithms**

- o **Recursive Tree Visualization**: Visualizing recursive calls as a tree to show how the problem is broken down.

- o **Time Complexity of Recursion**: Basic introduction to analyzing the time complexity of recursive functions using Big-O notation (e.g., factorial recursion as $O(n)$, Fibonacci as $O(2^n)$ for naive implementation).

- o **Memoization for Efficiency**: Introduction to memoization as a technique to optimize recursive functions, storing results of previous calculations to avoid redundant work.

o **Example with Memoization**: Implementing an optimized recursive Fibonacci sequence using a dictionary or list for memoization.

4. **Backtracking Basics**

o **What is Backtracking?**: Explanation of backtracking as a strategy to explore multiple solutions by recursively trying and "backing up" when a path fails.

o **Backtracking vs. Brute Force**: Understanding backtracking as a more efficient approach than brute force, pruning branches of the search tree that don't lead to solutions.

o **Typical Backtracking Problems**: Common applications of backtracking, such as puzzles (e.g., Sudoku), combinatorial problems, and pathfinding in mazes.

o **Real-World Example**: Using backtracking to find all valid arrangements of parentheses for a given number of pairs.

5. **Practical Recursive and Backtracking Problems**

o **Permutations and Combinations**:

▪ Writing a recursive function to generate all permutations of a list of items.

▪ Using backtracking to generate all combinations of a set of items.

o **Subset Sum Problem**: Finding subsets of a list that sum up to a target value, demonstrating how to backtrack by excluding elements that don't lead to solutions.

o **N-Queens Problem**: Solving the classic N-Queens problem by placing queens on a chessboard without them attacking each other, using backtracking to place each queen one by one and backtracking when conflicts arise.

o **Maze Solver**: Implementing a backtracking algorithm to solve a maze by recursively exploring paths until finding a solution or returning when paths reach dead ends.

o **Real-World Example**: Generating all possible letter combinations for a phone keypad input using recursion and backtracking to explore multiple possibilities.

6. **Advanced Concepts in Recursion**

o **Tail Recursion**: Explanation of tail recursion as a specific type of recursion where the recursive call is the final operation in the function, reducing memory overhead if supported by the language.

o **Recursive Depth and Limitations**: Discussing Python's recursion depth limit, sys.setrecursionlimit(), and when to consider iterative solutions over recursion for efficiency.

- o **Real-World Example**: Converting recursive algorithms to iterative ones for improved efficiency when handling large datasets (e.g., iterative Fibonacci calculation).

Real-World Examples and Projects

1. **Binary Search with Recursion**
   - o **Problem**: Write a recursive binary search algorithm that divides the sorted list in half each time to locate a target element.
   - o **Skills Practiced**: Divide-and-conquer recursion, base cases, and understanding time complexity ($O(\log n)$).
2. **Recursive Palindrome Checker**
   - o **Problem**: Write a function that uses recursion to check if a string is a palindrome (reads the same forwards and backwards).
   - o **Skills Practiced**: String manipulation, recursive base and recursive cases, and handling edge cases.
3. **Sudoku Solver**
   - o **Problem**: Implement a Sudoku solver using backtracking to fill in a grid with numbers 1-9,

ensuring that rows, columns, and sub-grids meet the puzzle constraints.

- ○ **Skills Practiced**: Recursive backtracking, constraint checking, and pruning invalid paths early.

4. **Combinatorial Sum**

- ○ **Problem**: Write a recursive function to find combinations of numbers that sum up to a given target value, allowing reuse of numbers.
- ○ **Skills Practiced**: Recursive backtracking, handling duplicates, and building combinations.

5. **Towers of Hanoi**

- ○ **Problem**: Solve the Towers of Hanoi puzzle using recursion, moving disks from one rod to another following the rules.
- ○ **Skills Practiced**: Recursion with multiple calls, base cases, and visualizing recursive depth through move steps.

Expanded Practice Problems

1. **Generating All Subsequences of a String**

- ○ **Problem**: Write a recursive function to generate all possible subsequences of a given string.

- o **Skills Practiced**: Recursive exploration, string manipulation, and understanding binary decisions (include/exclude).

2. **Knight's Tour Problem**

   - o **Problem**: Use backtracking to solve the Knight's Tour on a chessboard, where a knight must visit every square exactly once.

   - o **Skills Practiced**: Recursive backtracking, constraint-based movements, and visualizing paths.

3. **Word Search Puzzle Solver**

   - o **Problem**: Write a recursive function that searches for words in a grid by exploring all directions from each letter and backtracking on incorrect paths.

   - o **Skills Practiced**: Recursive backtracking, managing visited cells, and optimizing for large grids.

4. **Balanced Parentheses Generator**

   - o **Problem**: Use recursion and backtracking to generate all possible valid parentheses arrangements for a given number of pairs.

   - o **Skills Practiced**: Recursive backtracking, constraint checking, and generating balanced structures.

5. **Subset Partition Problem**

    o **Problem**: Write a recursive function to determine if a set can be partitioned into two subsets with equal sums.

    o **Skills Practiced**: Recursive backtracking, subset formation, and handling edge cases.

Mini Project: Recursive Directory Tree Explorer

Objective: Build a directory explorer that uses recursion to traverse all subdirectories and files in a given folder, generating a visual representation of the folder structure.

- **Problem Breakdown**:
  - o **Base Case and Recursive Case**: Define the base case as reaching a file (end of path) and the recursive case as entering each subdirectory.
  - o **File and Folder Identification**: Differentiate between files and folders using Python's os module.
  - o **Output**: Print the directory structure with indentation to show depth.
  - o **Skills Practiced**: Recursive function calls, base cases, handling nested folders, and visual representation of recursion.

By the end of this chapter, readers will have a solid understanding of recursion and backtracking, including base cases, recursive cases, and stack management. They'll be able to use recursion for a variety of practical tasks, from calculating factorials to solving combinatorial puzzles, and will understand when backtracking is effective for exploring multiple paths to a solution.

CHAPTER 19: SORTING AND SEARCHING ALGORITHMS

Sorting and searching are fundamental algorithmic techniques used in many areas of computer science. Efficient sorting and searching can significantly optimize data handling, making these algorithms vital in both basic and advanced programming. This chapter covers the basics of commonly used sorting algorithms (like bubble sort and merge sort), searching algorithms (like linear and binary search), and their applications in real-world problems.

Key Topics Covered

1. **Introduction to Sorting and Searching Algorithms**
   - **What Are Sorting and Searching?**: Explanation of sorting as organizing data in a specific order, and searching as locating data within a structure.
   - **Importance of Sorting and Searching**: Applications in data organization, retrieval, and optimization of data-driven applications.
   - **Algorithm Complexity**: Basic understanding of time complexity (Big-O notation) as it relates to the efficiency of sorting and searching algorithms.

Part 1: Sorting Algorithms

2. **Bubble Sort**

   o **How It Works**: Step-by-step explanation of how bubble sort repeatedly swaps adjacent elements if they are in the wrong order, "bubbling" the largest element to the end of the list in each pass.

   o **Time Complexity**: Explanation of why bubble sort has a time complexity of $O(n^2)$ in the average and worst cases.

   o **Pros and Cons**: Advantages of simplicity and ease of understanding, but poor efficiency on large datasets.

   o **Example**: Implementing bubble sort on an array of integers and displaying the sorted result.

3. **Selection Sort**

   o **How It Works**: Explanation of selection sort, where the algorithm repeatedly finds the smallest element in the unsorted portion of the list and moves it to the beginning.

   o **Time Complexity**: $O(n^2)$ complexity due to nested loops that compare and select minimum values.

   o **Pros and Cons**: Slightly better performance than bubble sort for smaller datasets but still inefficient for large datasets.

- o **Example**: Sorting an array of numbers using selection sort and printing the result.

4. **Insertion Sort**

  - o **How It Works**: Explanation of insertion sort, where elements are inserted one by one into the correct position within a growing sorted section.
  - o **Time Complexity**: $O(n^2)$ in the worst case, but more efficient than bubble or selection sort for nearly sorted arrays (best case $O(n)$).
  - o **Pros and Cons**: Good for small datasets and nearly sorted data, but inefficient on large, unordered datasets.
  - o **Example**: Sorting a small list of numbers using insertion sort.

5. **Merge Sort**

  - o **How It Works**: Explanation of merge sort as a divide-and-conquer algorithm that recursively splits the array into halves, sorts each half, and merges them back together.
  - o **Time Complexity**: $O(n \log n)$ for both the average and worst cases, making merge sort significantly more efficient than bubble, selection, and insertion sorts for larger datasets.
  - o **Pros and Cons**: Excellent for large datasets due to $O(n \log n)$ efficiency, but requires additional

memory for merging, which can be a limitation in memory-sensitive applications.

- ○ **Example**: Implementing merge sort on an array and printing each recursive merge step.

6. **Quick Sort**

- ○ **How It Works**: Explanation of quicksort as another divide-and-conquer algorithm, where an element (pivot) is chosen, and elements are partitioned around the pivot, recursively sorting smaller sections.

- ○ **Time Complexity**: $O(n \log n)$ on average, but $O(n^2)$ in the worst case if pivots are poorly chosen.

- ○ **Pros and Cons**: Very fast for large datasets with an average $O(n \log n)$ time complexity, but may perform poorly with unbalanced data or poorly chosen pivots.

- ○ **Example**: Implementing quicksort and showing the recursive partitioning process.

Part 2: Searching Algorithms

7. **Linear Search**

- ○ **How It Works**: Explanation of linear search as a simple technique where each element is checked sequentially until the target element is found.

o **Time Complexity**: O(n) for unsorted data, as each element may need to be examined.

o **Pros and Cons**: Simple and works on unsorted data but is inefficient for large datasets.

o **Example**: Using linear search to find an element in a list of numbers.

8. **Binary Search**

o **How It Works**: Explanation of binary search as a divide-and-conquer technique for sorted lists, where the list is divided in half, and the target element is compared to the middle element.

o **Time Complexity**: O(log n) due to halving the search range in each step, making it highly efficient for large, sorted datasets.

o **Requirements**: Works only on sorted data, requiring an initial sorting step if the list is unordered.

o **Example**: Using binary search to locate a specific number in a sorted list, demonstrating each halving step.

9. **Practical Applications of Sorting and Searching**

o **Data Organization**: Sorting algorithms are essential for preparing data for efficient access, such as sorting user lists or product inventories.

- o **Efficient Retrieval**: Combining sorting with binary search for fast lookup operations, such as in databases or large datasets.
- o **Real-World Example**: Creating an application to search for student records based on ID, requiring sorting and binary search for efficiency.

Real-World Examples and Projects

1. **Contact List Sorter**
   - o **Problem**: Create a program to organize a contact list by last name, allowing users to search for contacts by name.
   - o **Skills Practiced**: Using sorting (e.g., quicksort or merge sort) and binary search for efficient lookups.

2. **Library Book Finder**
   - o **Problem**: Write a program that sorts a list of books by title or author and allows users to search for specific books.
   - o **Skills Practiced**: Sorting by different attributes and implementing binary search.

3. **Inventory Management System**
   - o **Problem**: Design an inventory management system that sorts items by price or quantity and allows users to search for items within a specific range.

- o **Skills Practiced**: Sorting, binary search, and using algorithms for data management.

4. **Product Price Sorter**
   - o **Problem**: Develop a program that sorts a list of products by price (low to high or high to low) and allows users to search for products within a price range.
   - o **Skills Practiced**: Sorting algorithms and range search using binary search.

5. **Student Grade Organizer**
   - o **Problem**: Implement a system that sorts student grades in ascending or descending order and allows the user to search for students with specific grades.
   - o **Skills Practiced**: Sorting, binary search, and condition-based search.

Expanded Practice Problems

1. **Top K Elements Finder**
   - o **Problem**: Find the top K highest scores in a list using sorting and binary search.
   - o **Skills Practiced**: Sorting, selecting specific elements, and using search to locate specific scores.

2. **Anagram Finder**

- o **Problem**: Given a list of words, find all anagrams by sorting each word and grouping them by sorted characters.
- o **Skills Practiced**: Sorting within search, data manipulation, and grouping results.

3. **Number Frequency Counter**
   - o **Problem**: Sort a list of numbers and find the most frequent number using binary search for fast access.
   - o **Skills Practiced**: Sorting, searching, and frequency counting.

4. **String Matching in Sorted List**
   - o **Problem**: Given a sorted list of strings, search for strings that match a specific prefix using binary search.
   - o **Skills Practiced**: Binary search, prefix matching, and efficient data retrieval.

5. **Movie Recommendation System**
   - o **Problem**: Sort movies by ratings and use binary search to filter movies within a specific rating range for recommendations.
   - o **Skills Practiced**: Sorting, binary search, and filtering based on conditions.

Mini Project: E-commerce Price Filter

Objective: Build a simple e-commerce price filter that sorts products by price and allows users to search for products within a specified price range.

- **Problem Breakdown**:
    - **Sort Products**: Sort the list of products by price using an efficient sorting algorithm like quicksort or merge sort.
    - **Binary Search for Range**: Use binary search to quickly find the starting and ending indices for products within the specified price range.
    - **Display Results**: Show all products within the chosen price range in ascending order.
    - **Skills Practiced**: Sorting, binary search, and conditional data filtering.

By the end of this chapter, readers will understand the basics of sorting and searching algorithms, including bubble sort, merge sort, quicksort, linear search, and binary search. They'll be able to apply these algorithms to real-world tasks, optimizing data handling, and performing efficient lookups, which are crucial skills for both everyday programming and technical interviews.

CHAPTER 20: DATA STRUCTURES – STACKS AND QUEUES

Stacks and queues are fundamental data structures in computer science, providing efficient ways to handle ordered data. Both structures follow specific rules for inserting and removing elements, making them ideal for a wide range of applications. This chapter covers how to implement and use stacks and queues in Python, along with practical examples to demonstrate their real-world uses.

Key Topics Covered

Part 1: Stacks

1. **Introduction to Stacks**
   - **Definition of a Stack**: Explanation of stacks as a Last-In-First-Out (LIFO) data structure where the most recently added element is the first to be removed.

- o **Real-World Analogies**: Using a stack of plates where you add (push) and remove (pop) plates from the top as a real-world analogy.

- o **Applications of Stacks**: Common uses, such as function call management in recursion, backtracking, and undo operations in applications.

2. **Implementing a Stack in Python**

- o **Using Lists**: Implementing a stack using Python's list with append() for pushing elements and pop() for popping elements.

- o **Basic Stack Operations**:
  - **Push**: Adding an element to the top of the stack.
  - **Pop**: Removing and returning the top element of the stack.
  - **Peek**: Returning the top element without removing it.
  - **isEmpty**: Checking if the stack is empty.

- o **Example Implementation**: Building a stack class using Python lists and implementing the basic operations.

3. **Practical Applications of Stacks**

- o **Balancing Parentheses**: Using a stack to check if a string of parentheses is balanced, ensuring every opening bracket has a corresponding closing bracket.

- o **Undo Functionality in Text Editors**: Implementing an undo feature where recent actions are pushed onto a stack and can be undone by popping the stack.
- o **Reverse a String**: Using a stack to reverse a string by pushing each character onto the stack and then popping characters off.
- o **Real-World Example**: Implementing a stack-based calculator that evaluates mathematical expressions (e.g., postfix notation).

4. **Advanced Stack Techniques**
   - o **Implementing Stacks with Deques**: Using Python's collections.deque for efficient stack operations, as deque provides O(1) complexity for both appending and popping.
   - o **Handling Stack Overflow and Underflow**: Explanation of stack overflow (when adding to a full stack) and underflow (when removing from an empty stack) and handling these cases in a fixed-size stack.
   - o **Real-World Example**: Using stacks to navigate back and forth through browser history, with a back stack and a forward stack.

Part 2: Queues

5. **Introduction to Queues**

   ○ **Definition of a Queue**: Explanation of queues as a First-In-First-Out (FIFO) data structure where the first added element is the first to be removed.

   ○ **Real-World Analogies**: A queue at a ticket counter where people are served in the order they arrived.

   ○ **Applications of Queues**: Uses in task scheduling, buffering, real-time processing, and managing tasks in multi-threaded environments.

6. **Implementing a Queue in Python**

   ○ **Using Lists**: Implementing a queue using Python lists with append() to add to the rear and pop(0) to remove from the front, though this approach is not optimal for large queues.

   ○ **Using collections.deque for Efficient Queues**: Using deque to implement queues efficiently, as deque supports O(1) complexity for both append and pop operations from either end.

   ○ **Basic Queue Operations**:

      ▪ **Enqueue**: Adding an element to the rear of the queue.

      ▪ **Dequeue**: Removing and returning the front element of the queue.

      ▪ **Peek**: Returning the front element without removing it.

- **isEmpty**: Checking if the queue is empty.
  - **Example Implementation**: Building a queue class using deque and implementing the basic operations.

7. **Practical Applications of Queues**
   - **Task Scheduling**: Using queues to manage tasks in order, where each task is processed in the order it was added (e.g., printing jobs in a print queue).
   - **Breadth-First Search (BFS)**: Applying queues in BFS for graph traversal, processing each node level by level.
   - **Customer Service Simulation**: Using a queue to simulate a line of customers in a bank, where each customer is served in order.
   - **Real-World Example**: Implementing a message queue where each message is processed in the order it was received.

8. **Variants of Queues**
   - **Circular Queue**: Explanation of circular queues where the queue wraps around, useful for fixed-size queues (e.g., in buffering).
   - **Double-Ended Queue (Deque)**: Explanation of deques, allowing insertion and deletion at both ends, and showing practical cases where both ends need to be accessible.

○ **Priority Queue**: Introduction to priority queues where elements are ordered based on priority rather than insertion order, using Python's heapq module.

○ **Real-World Example**: Implementing a priority queue for scheduling tasks by urgency, where higher-priority tasks are processed first.

Real-World Examples and Projects

1. **Browser Navigation (Stack-Based)**

   ○ **Problem**: Create a program that simulates browser navigation, allowing users to go back and forward between pages using two stacks (back and forward stacks).

   ○ **Skills Practiced**: Stack operations, handling multiple stacks, and managing history.

2. **Task Scheduling System (Queue-Based)**

   ○ **Problem**: Implement a task scheduling system where tasks are added to a queue and processed in the order they arrived.

   ○ **Skills Practiced**: Queue operations, task management, and real-time processing.

3. **Balanced Parentheses Checker**

o   **Problem**: Write a function that uses a stack to check if an expression with parentheses (and possibly other brackets) is balanced.

o   **Skills Practiced**: Stack operations, handling complex conditions, and parsing strings.

4. **Customer Service Simulation (Queue-Based)**

o   **Problem**: Simulate a customer service line where each new customer is added to the queue, and each customer is served in FIFO order.

o   **Skills Practiced**: Queue operations, simulating real-world systems, and managing FIFO logic.

5. **Expression Evaluator (Postfix Notation)**

o   **Problem**: Implement a stack-based calculator that evaluates mathematical expressions written in postfix notation.

o   **Skills Practiced**: Stack operations, handling mathematical operations, and parsing expressions.

Expanded Practice Problems

1. **Palindrome Checker**

o   **Problem**: Use a stack to check if a word or phrase is a palindrome by comparing characters in reverse order.

o **Skills Practiced**: Stack operations, string manipulation, and conditional checks.

2. **Ticket Counter Simulation (Queue-Based)**

   o **Problem**: Simulate a ticket counter with a queue where people line up for tickets, and each person is served in order.

   o **Skills Practiced**: Queue operations and simulating FIFO in real-life scenarios.

3. **Printer Queue Management**

   o **Problem**: Implement a printer queue where multiple jobs are queued, with priority given to jobs based on urgency.

   o **Skills Practiced**: Priority queue implementation, task management, and handling job orders.

4. **Directory Traversal (Depth-First Search)**

   o **Problem**: Use a stack to implement depth-first traversal of a directory, listing all files and subdirectories.

   o **Skills Practiced**: Stack operations, file system traversal, and recursion.

5. **Simulation of Call Center (Queue-Based)**

   o **Problem**: Simulate a call center where calls are added to a queue and each agent processes calls in the order received.

- o **Skills Practiced**: Queue management, task scheduling, and handling real-time processes.

Mini Project: Real-Time Messaging Queue

Objective: Build a real-time messaging queue where messages are received, queued, and processed in the order they arrive.

- **Problem Breakdown**:
    - o **Queue Implementation**: Use a queue data structure to manage messages received.
    - o **Processing Messages**: Dequeue and process each message in order.
    - o **Prioritization Option**: Include an option to prioritize urgent messages using a priority queue if desired.
    - o **Skills Practiced**: Queue operations, real-time processing, and managing multiple message types.

By the end of this chapter, readers will have a comprehensive understanding of stacks and queues, including how to implement them and apply them in real-world scenarios. They'll know how to choose the right data structure based on the problem requirements (LIFO vs. FIFO) and will be prepared to implement more complex algorithms that rely on these structures.

CHAPTER 21: BUILDING A COMMAND-LINE INTERFACE (CLI) APPLICATION

Command-Line Interface (CLI) applications are text-based programs that interact with users via the command line, offering a straightforward and efficient way to build functional applications without the complexity of graphical interfaces. In this chapter, we'll walk through designing, coding, and refining a CLI application to gain practical, hands-on experience. We'll focus on creating a fully functional task manager that allows users to add, update, and delete tasks directly from the terminal.

Key Topics Covered

1. **Introduction to CLI Applications**

    o **What is a CLI Application?**: Explanation of CLI applications as text-based programs that operate through the command line, often used for automation, data processing, and tool-building.

- **Advantages of CLI Applications**: Fast, lightweight, and resource-efficient with minimal dependencies, making them ideal for automation tasks.
- **Designing CLI Applications**: Overview of planning and structuring commands, handling user input, and providing feedback.

2. **Setting Up the Development Environment**

- **Python Basics for CLI**: Ensuring Python is installed and setting up the environment for CLI development.
- **Libraries for CLI Applications**: Introduction to libraries like argparse, click, and sys for handling command-line arguments, although the primary focus will be on argparse for simplicity.
- **Project Folder Structure**: Organizing the project folder, including directories for core code, tests, and configuration files.

3. **Planning the Task Manager CLI**

- **Defining Application Requirements**: Outline of core functionality, such as adding, viewing, updating, and deleting tasks.
- **Designing Commands**: Specifying key commands (add, list, update, delete) and understanding how each command will function.

- o **User Stories and Flow**: Brief user stories to identify how users will interact with each feature, e.g., "As a user, I want to add a task with a due date so that I can keep track of deadlines."
- o **Data Storage**: Deciding on a storage format (e.g., JSON, CSV, or a simple text file) for saving task data persistently.

Part 1: Implementing the Task Manager CLI Application

4. **Setting Up the argparse Framework**
   - o **Introduction to argparse**: Using argparse to create and parse command-line arguments.
   - o **Defining Commands**: Adding commands for each task manager feature (add, list, update, delete) and structuring arguments and options.
   - o **Real-World Example**: Setting up argparse to handle a simple "add task" command with options for task name and due date.

5. **Implementing Core Functionality**
   - o **Adding Tasks**:
     - ▪ Writing a function to add tasks, accepting arguments like task name, description, priority, and due date.
     - ▪ Saving tasks to a JSON file, providing a simple, readable format for data storage.

- o **Listing Tasks**:
  - Implementing a list command to display all tasks.
  - Providing options to filter tasks (e.g., by priority or due date) and format the output.
- o **Updating Tasks**:
  - Writing a function to modify task attributes (e.g., change the due date or priority).
  - Handling edge cases, such as updating non-existent tasks or invalid input.
- o **Deleting Tasks**:
  - Implementing a delete command to remove tasks by ID or name.
  - Providing confirmation before deletion to avoid accidental data loss.
- o **Example**: Demonstrating each command with sample tasks, showing how the command syntax works.

Part 2: Enhancing the CLI with Additional Features

6. **Error Handling and Validation**
   - o **Input Validation**: Ensuring users enter valid inputs (e.g., correct date format, non-empty task names).

- o **Error Messages**: Providing user-friendly error messages for invalid commands, missing arguments, or other issues.

- o **Handling File Errors**: Managing errors when reading or writing to files, such as file not found or permission issues.

- o **Real-World Example**: Handling common errors gracefully, with feedback to guide users toward correct usage.

7. **Improving Usability with Help and Feedback**

- o **Help and Usage Messages**: Using argparse to automatically generate help text for each command.

- o **Feedback Messages**: Displaying confirmation messages for each operation (e.g., "Task added successfully") and notifying users of failed operations.

- o **Command Aliases and Shortcuts**: Creating shorter command aliases (like rm for delete) for quicker usage and convenience.

- o **Example**: Testing the usability by running each command with help options, checking for clear descriptions and feedback.

8. **Storing and Managing Task Data**

- o **Data Structure for Tasks**: Structuring each task as a dictionary with attributes like ID, name, description, priority, and due date.

- o **Using JSON for Data Storage**: Storing tasks in a JSON file for persistent storage across sessions and reading from it when loading tasks.

- o **Loading and Saving Data Efficiently**: Implementing functions to read and write task data at appropriate times (e.g., loading at startup, saving after each modification).

- o **Example**: Demonstrating how tasks are stored in JSON and retrieving tasks at startup.

Part 3: Advanced Features and Final Enhancements

9. **Adding Task Sorting and Filtering**

- o **Sorting Tasks by Attribute**: Allowing users to sort tasks by attributes like due date, priority, or creation date.

- o **Filtering Tasks**: Adding options to filter tasks by priority level, completion status, or due date range.

- o **Real-World Example**: Filtering and sorting tasks to demonstrate how these features enhance usability.

10. **Marking Tasks as Completed**

o **Adding a Completion Attribute**: Adding a completion status to each task (e.g., completed: True).

o **Marking as Complete**: Implementing a command to mark tasks as complete and updating the JSON data file.

o **Listing Completed Tasks**: Providing options to display only completed tasks or only incomplete tasks.

o **Example**: Showing how to mark a task as complete and verify the change in the task list.

11. **Task Reminders and Due Date Notifications**

o **Setting Due Dates**: Adding due dates to tasks and implementing logic to check for upcoming or overdue tasks.

o **Generating Notifications**: Displaying reminders or alerts for tasks due within a specified timeframe (e.g., due within 24 hours).

o **Real-World Example**: Listing tasks with upcoming due dates and using visual markers to distinguish overdue tasks.

12. **Saving Task History and Archiving**

o **Archiving Completed Tasks**: Moving completed tasks to an archive file or separate JSON structure to keep the active task list uncluttered.

o **Viewing Archived Tasks**: Providing a command to view archived tasks, enabling users to see past activity.

o **Real-World Example**: Demonstrating how to archive completed tasks and retrieve archived data as needed.

Part 4: Testing, Refinement, and Documentation

13. Testing the CLI Application

o **Unit Testing**: Writing unit tests for each function (e.g., adding, updating, deleting tasks) using Python's unittest module.

o **Command-Line Testing**: Testing commands manually to ensure all interactions work as expected, handling edge cases like invalid inputs.

o **Error and Edge Case Testing**: Testing scenarios such as adding duplicate tasks, deleting non-existent tasks, and handling empty lists.

o **Example**: Running a suite of tests to validate the robustness of the application.

14. Documenting the Task Manager

o **Creating a User Guide**: Writing clear documentation for each command, including descriptions, options, and examples.

- o **Help and Usage Documentation**: Ensuring argparse provides comprehensive help text that covers all commands and options.

- o **Example Documentation**: Sample documentation for a README file, detailing the purpose, setup instructions, and usage of each command.

15. **Packaging and Deployment**

- o **Packaging the Application**: Using setuptools to package the CLI application, making it installable and executable from the command line.

- o **Adding Entry Points**: Setting up an entry point in setup.py for running the task manager directly from the terminal.

- o **Distributing and Installing**: Creating a distributable package and demonstrating how users can install and run the application.

- o **Example**: Installing the packaged application and running it on a new system to verify correct installation and functionality.

Final Project: Task Manager CLI Application

Objective: Develop a fully functional command-line task manager that allows users to add, view, update, delete, and manage tasks with options for sorting, filtering, and marking tasks as complete.

- **Core Functionality**:
  - ○ Adding, updating, listing, and deleting tasks.
  - ○ Sorting and filtering tasks by attributes like priority and due date.
  - ○ Marking tasks as complete and archiving completed tasks.
- **Advanced Features**:
  - ○ Due date notifications for tasks nearing deadlines.
  - ○ Task archiving to keep the active task list organized.
  - ○ Persistent storage of tasks in a JSON file for long-term use.
- **Testing and Documentation**:
  - ○ Unit testing for each feature and thorough command-line testing.
  - ○ User guide and README documentation, including example commands.

By completing this chapter, readers will have designed, implemented, and refined a comprehensive CLI application from scratch, gaining experience in structured coding, command-line interaction, data persistence, and user-oriented design. This final project solidifies key skills in Python, making them ready to build more complex applications and interfaces.

CHAPTER 22: TESTING AND DEBUGGING CLI APPLICATIONS

Testing and debugging are essential for creating reliable, error-free Command-Line Interface (CLI) applications. This chapter covers testing CLI applications to ensure functionality and prevent errors. We'll explore techniques using Python's unittest module for core function testing, mock user inputs, and command-line argument testing. We'll also dive into debugging techniques using Python's built-in debugger (pdb), logging to troubleshoot issues, and setting up Continuous Integration (CI) with GitHub Actions to automate testing.

Part 1: Unit Testing CLI Applications

Importance of Testing CLI Applications

Testing is vital for CLI applications because users rely on them for tasks that often involve data manipulation, system operations, or automated workflows. Uncaught errors or unexpected behavior can

compromise productivity, data integrity, and user trust. Testing
ensures:

- **Reliability**: The application works as expected across
  different commands and scenarios.
- **Error Detection**: Bugs are caught early, reducing the risk
  of user-facing issues.
- **Code Maintainability**: Regular testing helps maintain code
  quality and functionality as the application evolves.

Using unittest for Core Function Testing

Python's unittest module is well-suited for CLI application testing.
It provides a framework for creating, organizing, and running test
cases. With unittest, you can isolate core functions in your CLI
application and ensure each works independently before
integrating them into the command structure.

1. **Setting Up Tests**: Create a test file (e.g.,
   test_task_manager.py) in your project directory and import
   the CLI module or specific functions.

python

import unittest

```python
from task_manager import TaskManager   # Example CLI
module
```

2. **Creating Test Cases**: Use the TestCase class to define methods that test specific functions or behaviors. For example, if your CLI application has an add_task function, create a test case to verify it adds tasks correctly.

python

```python
class TestTaskManager(unittest.TestCase):
    def test_add_task(self):
        task_manager = TaskManager()
        task_manager.add_task("Write Chapter", "2024-11-30")
        self.assertIn("Write Chapter", task_manager.get_all_tasks())
```

3. **Running Tests**: Run tests from the command line to see if they pass or fail:

bash

```bash
python -m unittest test_task_manager.py
```

This command will execute all test cases in test_task_manager.py, displaying a summary of passed and failed tests.

Validating Command Inputs

Testing command inputs is crucial for ensuring your CLI application handles user-provided data accurately. You can add validation tests to check:

- If inputs are in the expected format (e.g., correct date format).
- If required fields are provided (e.g., task name).
- If invalid inputs trigger appropriate error messages.

python

```python
def test_add_task_invalid_date(self):
    task_manager = TaskManager()
    with self.assertRaises(ValueError):
        task_manager.add_task("Write Chapter", "invalid-date")
```

This test checks that add_task raises a ValueError if the date is in an invalid format.

Mocking User Input and Simulating Command-Line Arguments

To test user inputs and simulate command-line arguments, use the unittest.mock module. This approach allows you to test user-driven commands without requiring actual user interaction.

1. **Mocking Input**: Mocking lets you simulate inputs and test how functions handle them. For example, mock user input for interactive commands.

python

```
from unittest.mock import patch

@patch("builtins.input", side_effect=["Test Task", "2024-12-01"])
def test_add_task_interactive(self, mock_input):
    task_manager = TaskManager()
    task_manager.add_task_interactive()   # Assuming an interactive add function
    self.assertIn("Test Task", task_manager.get_all_tasks())
```

2. **Simulating Command-Line Arguments**: Use patch to mock sys.argv and simulate command-line arguments, allowing you to test full command executions.

python

```
@patch("sys.argv", ["task_manager.py", "add", "Test Task", "2024-12-01"])
def test_command_line_add_task(self):
    task_manager = TaskManager()
```

task_manager.run() # Assuming a main run function that processes commands

self.assertIn("Test Task", task_manager.get_all_tasks())

This test simulates running the add command directly from the command line with specific arguments, helping ensure command handling is accurate.

Part 2: Debugging Techniques for CLI Applications

Common Issues in CLI Applications

CLI applications can encounter various issues, such as:

- **Invalid Inputs**: Users may enter unexpected inputs, leading to crashes or misbehavior.
- **Incorrect Argument Parsing**: Errors in argument parsing can cause the application to misinterpret commands.
- **File Errors**: If the application uses file storage, file-related issues (e.g., missing files, incorrect permissions) can disrupt functionality.

Effective debugging techniques help quickly identify and resolve these issues.

Using Python's pdb Debugger

Python's pdb module is a powerful tool for debugging code line-by-line. You can insert pdb.set_trace() at specific points in your code to pause execution and interactively inspect variable values and control flow.

1. **Setting a Breakpoint**: Insert pdb.set_trace() in the function you want to inspect.

   python

   import pdb

   ```python
   def add_task(name, due_date):
       pdb.set_trace()  # Pauses here for inspection
       task = {"name": name, "due_date": due_date}
       tasks.append(task)
   ```

2. **Running and Inspecting**: Run the program and execute commands in the debugger to check variable values and control flow. Common commands include:
   - n (next): Executes the next line.
   - s (step): Steps into a function.
   - p (print): Prints the value of a variable.

Adding Logging to Track Actions

Logging is useful for tracking the application's actions and recording issues as they occur. Python's logging module allows you to write logs to the console or files for troubleshooting.

1. **Setting Up Logging**: Initialize a logger in your application's main module.

python

import logging

logging.basicConfig(level=logging.INFO, filename="task_manager.log")

2. **Adding Log Messages**: Log important events or errors. For example, log successful task additions and input errors.

python

```
def add_task(name, due_date):
    try:
        # Attempt to add task
        task = {"name": name, "due_date": due_date}
        tasks.append(task)
        logging.info(f"Task added: {name}")
    except ValueError as e:
        logging.error(f"Error adding task: {e}")
```

3. **Reading Logs**: Check the log file (task_manager.log) to analyze recorded messages and troubleshoot recurring issues.

Part 3: Automated Testing with CI/CD

Introduction to Continuous Integration for CLI Applications

Continuous Integration (CI) ensures that code changes are automatically tested as they're pushed to a repository. This process helps maintain code quality by catching issues early. GitHub Actions is a popular tool for automating CI workflows in GitHub repositories.

Setting Up GitHub Actions for Automated Testing

1. **Creating a GitHub Actions Workflow**: In your repository, create a new folder called .github/workflows/. Inside, add a YAML file for your workflow (e.g., ci.yml).

2. **Defining the Workflow**: Configure the workflow to run tests on each push. The workflow example below installs Python, sets up dependencies, and runs your unittest tests.

yaml

```yaml
name: CLI Application CI

on: [push, pull_request]

jobs:
  test:
    runs-on: ubuntu-latest
    steps:
      - name: Checkout code
        uses: actions/checkout@v2

      - name: Set up Python
        uses: actions/setup-python@v2
        with:
          python-version: '3.8'

      - name: Install dependencies
        run: |
          python -m pip install --upgrade pip
          pip install -r requirements.txt

      - name: Run tests
        run: python -m unittest discover -s tests
```

3. **Running the Workflow**: Commit and push this file to trigger the GitHub Actions workflow. Check the "Actions" tab in GitHub to monitor the status of your workflow.

Example CI Pipeline for CLI Application Testing

Here's a practical example of how a CI pipeline validates your CLI application:

- **Test**: Executes the test suite with each push or pull request to ensure new code doesn't break existing functionality.
- **Build**: (Optional) Builds the CLI application package to confirm it installs correctly.
- **Deploy**: (Optional) Deploys a successful build to a test environment or artifact storage, making it available for further testing.

This chapter covered crucial aspects of testing and debugging CLI applications to ensure functionality, reliability, and maintainability. With unittest, pdb, logging, and automated CI/CD workflows, you now have a toolkit for creating and maintaining robust CLI applications that deliver dependable, error-free performance. Let me know if you'd like further examples or additional debugging scenarios!

CHAPTER 23: ENHANCING THE USER EXPERIENCE IN CLI APPLICATIONS

A great Command-Line Interface (CLI) application doesn't just perform tasks; it interacts with users smoothly and intuitively. In this chapter, we'll discuss methods for enhancing the user experience in CLI applications, including customizing feedback, adding input validation, and creating user configuration files. Each of these elements will improve the usability, clarity, and personalization of your CLI application.

Part 1: Improving Command-Line Feedback

Effective feedback helps users understand what's happening at each stage of their interaction with the CLI application. This feedback can include clear status messages, progress indicators, and color-coding for readability.

Customizing Feedback for a Smooth User Experience

1. **Clear Status Messages**: CLI applications should provide concise and informative feedback for each command. For example:

    o Displaying a success message when a task is completed.

    o Providing error messages for issues such as invalid inputs or command syntax.

python

```
def add_task(name):
    # Task addition logic here
    print(f"Task '{name}' has been successfully added.")
```

2. **User-Friendly Command Prompts**: Use prompts that guide the user on the next action, especially in interactive applications. Instead of a generic input, use informative text to help users understand what's expected:

python

```
task_name = input("Enter the task name (or 'q' to quit): ")
```

3. **Using Emojis and Symbols**: Emojis and symbols can make feedback more visually engaging and easier to understand:

- ○ ✅ for success.

- ○ ✖ for errors.

- ○ **i**☐ for information.

python

print("✅ Task completed successfully.")

Using Color-Coded Output with colorama

Adding color to command-line output can improve readability by highlighting important information. The colorama library is commonly used for color coding in Python CLI applications.

1. **Installing Colorama**:

bash

pip install colorama

2. **Using Colorama in Your CLI Application**:
   - ○ Import colorama and initialize it at the start of the application.
   - ○ Apply colors to text using Fore, Back, and Style.

python

```
from colorama import Fore, Style, init
init(autoreset=True)


def add_task(name):
    print(Fore.GREEN + f"✓ Task '{name}' has been
successfully added.")
    print(Style.RESET_ALL)
```

3. **Common Color Applications**:
   - o **Green** for success messages.
   - o **Red** for error messages.
   - o **Yellow** for warnings or pending actions.
   - o **Blue** or **cyan** for informational text.

Using color coding consistently across your CLI application helps users quickly identify the nature of each message.

Providing Progress Indicators and Structured Data Output

For long-running operations, progress indicators reassure users that the process is ongoing.

1. **Using a Simple Loading Indicator**: For tasks like data processing or network requests, display a "Loading..." message with a rotating symbol to show ongoing progress.

python

```
import itertools, sys, time

def loading_indicator():
    for symbol in itertools.cycle(['|', '/', '-', '\\']):
        sys.stdout.write(f"\rLoading... {symbol}")
        sys.stdout.flush()
        time.sleep(0.1)
```

2. **Displaying Progress Bars with tqdm**: The tqdm library is useful for displaying progress bars.

bash

```
pip install tqdm
python
```

```
from tqdm import tqdm
import time

for i in tqdm(range(100)):
    time.sleep(0.1)  # Simulating a task
```

3. **Structured Data Output with Tables**: For complex data (e.g., lists of tasks), use a structured table format to

improve readability. Libraries like tabulate help with generating table-style outputs.

bash

```
pip install tabulate
```

python

```
from tabulate import tabulate

tasks = [
    {"Name": "Write Chapter", "Due": "2024-11-30", "Priority": "High"},
    {"Name": "Test CLI", "Due": "2024-12-01", "Priority": "Medium"},
]

print(tabulate(tasks, headers="keys", tablefmt="fancy_grid"))
```

Output:

mathematica

| Name | Due | Priority |

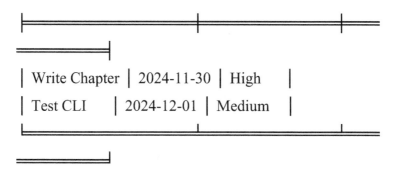

| Write Chapter | 2024-11-30 | High |
| Test CLI | 2024-12-01 | Medium |

Part 2: Adding User Input Validation and Error Handling

Validating user input and providing clear error messages are essential for a robust CLI application.

Validating User Input for Smoother Interactions

Input validation ensures that users enter data in the correct format, minimizing runtime errors and improving reliability.

1. **Basic Validation**: Use conditional checks to validate common inputs, such as non-empty task names or correct date formats.

python

```
import re

def validate_date(date_str):
    if not re.match(r"\d{4}-\d{2}-\d{2}", date_str):
```

```python
print(Fore.RED + "✖ Invalid date format. Use YYYY-MM-DD.")
    return False
return True
```

2. **Validating Command-Line Arguments**: If your CLI application accepts command-line arguments, validate them before processing.

python

```python
import sys

if len(sys.argv) < 2:
    print(Fore.RED + "✖ Error: Missing task name.")
    sys.exit(1)
```

Providing Descriptive Error Messages to Guide Users

Clear error messages help users understand and resolve issues. A good error message should:

- Explain the error.
- Suggest corrective action.

python

```
def add_task(name):
    if not name:
        print(Fore.RED + "✘ Error: Task name cannot be empty.")
        print("Please provide a name for the task.")
        return
```

Using Data Validation Libraries (cerberus and marshmallow)

For complex input validation, libraries like cerberus or marshmallow can define schemas to enforce rules on data structure and format.

1. **Installing and Using cerberus**:

    bash

    pip install cerberus
    python

    from cerberus import Validator

    schema = {'name': {'type': 'string', 'empty': False}, 'due_date': {'type': 'string', 'regex': r'\d{4}-\d{2}-\d{2}'}}
    validator = Validator(schema)

    def add_task(task):

```python
    if validator.validate(task):
        # Add task logic
        print("Task added!")
    else:
        print(Fore.RED + f"Error: {validator.errors}")
```

2. **Using marshmallow for Advanced Validation**:

bash

pip install marshmallow
python

```python
from marshmallow import Schema, fields, ValidationError

class TaskSchema(Schema):
    name = fields.String(required=True)
    due_date = fields.Date(required=True, format="%Y-%m-%d")

task_schema = TaskSchema()

def add_task(task):
    try:
        task_schema.load(task)
        print("Task added!")
```

```
except ValidationError as e:
    print(Fore.RED + f"Validation error: {e.messages}")
```

Part 3: Creating a User Configuration File

Configuration files allow users to personalize and save their preferences, such as default output formats or sorting options. JSON and YAML are common formats for configuration files in CLI applications.

Allowing Users to Personalize Their Experience

1. **Defining User Preferences**: Identify customizable options (e.g., color preferences, default sorting order) and add them to the configuration file.
2. **Loading Configuration at Runtime**: When the application starts, load the configuration file and apply settings accordingly.

Setting Default Preferences for Commands and Output

Create a dictionary for default preferences and update it with user-defined preferences from the configuration file.

python

```python
import json

default_config = {
    "display_colors": True,
    "default_sort": "priority",
    "date_format": "%Y-%m-%d"
}

def load_config():
    try:
        with open("config.json") as f:
            user_config = json.load(f)
            default_config.update(user_config)
    except FileNotFoundError:
        print("No configuration file found. Using defaults.")

load_config()
```

Saving Configurations in JSON or YAML Formats

1. **Creating the Configuration File**:
   - Prompt the user to customize preferences when the application is first run, and save these preferences to a file.

```python
python
```

```python
with open("config.json", "w") as f:
    json.dump(default_config, f)
```

2. **Using YAML for Complex Configurations**: For more complex configurations, use YAML for readability.

```bash
bash
```

```bash
pip install pyyaml
python
```

```python
import yaml
```

```python
def load_config():
    with open("config.yaml") as f:
        return yaml.safe_load(f)
```

Enhancing the user experience in CLI applications involves more than just functionality. By implementing color-coded feedback, progress indicators, input validation, and configuration options, you create a user-friendly and polished CLI experience. These features help make the application intuitive, responsive, and adaptable to each user's preferences.

CHAPTER 24: ADVANCED FEATURES AND EXTENSIONS FOR CLI APPLICATIONS

To develop sophisticated and secure Command-Line Interface (CLI) applications, advanced features such as authentication, interactive menus, and extensible plugin architectures are invaluable. This chapter will cover implementing these features, enabling users to build powerful and flexible CLI applications. By adding authentication, interactive menus, and plugin support, you'll elevate the user experience and functionality of your CLI tool.

Part 1: Adding Authentication to CLI Applications

Authentication provides secure access to CLI applications, especially those that connect to external services or handle sensitive data. Implementing authentication enhances security, protects data, and ensures that only authorized users can access specific functionalities.

Implementing Basic Authentication for Secure Access

1. **Username and Password Authentication**: Basic authentication requires users to enter a username and password to access the application.

    o **Setting Up a Basic Authentication System**: Define a simple login function that validates credentials.

python

```python
import getpass

def authenticate(username, password):
    # Hardcoded example; replace with database or API call
in production
    if username == "admin" and password == "secret":
    print("✓ Authentication successful")
    return True
    else:
    print("✗ Invalid credentials")
```

```
        return False
```

```
username = input("Username: ")
password = getpass.getpass("Password: ")
authenticate(username, password)
```

2. **Storing Hashed Passwords**: Never store passwords as plain text. Instead, use password hashing with libraries like bcrypt or hashlib.

python

```
from bcrypt import hashpw, gensalt, checkpw
```

```
hashed_password = hashpw("secret".encode(), gensalt())
```

Using OAuth or API Tokens for Secure External Connections
OAuth and API tokens provide secure access to external services like GitHub, Google APIs, or custom RESTful APIs.

1. **OAuth Authentication**: OAuth is a secure authorization standard that allows third-party services to access user data without sharing passwords. Use libraries like requests-oauthlib to integrate OAuth.

bash

```
pip install requests requests-oauthlib
python

from requests_oauthlib import OAuth2Session

client_id = "YOUR_CLIENT_ID"
client_secret = "YOUR_CLIENT_SECRET"
authorization_base_url                              =
"https://example.com/oauth/authorize"
token_url = "https://example.com/oauth/token"

oauth = OAuth2Session(client_id)
authorization_url,              state              =
oauth.authorization_url(authorization_base_url)
print("Visit this URL to authorize:", authorization_url)
```

2. **API Token Authentication**: API tokens allow applications to authenticate without user credentials. Store API tokens securely and pass them in headers for secure access.

```
python

import os
import requests
```

```python
api_token = os.getenv("API_TOKEN")  # Store token as an
environment variable
headers = {"Authorization": f"Bearer {api_token}"}
response = requests.get("https://api.example.com/data",
headers=headers)
```

Managing Sensitive Data with Environment Variables and Secret Storage

Sensitive data, such as passwords, API keys, and tokens, should be stored securely.

1. **Using Environment Variables**: Load sensitive data from environment variables to prevent hardcoding.

   python

   ```python
   import os
   api_key = os.getenv("API_KEY")
   ```

2. **Using .env Files with python-dotenv**: .env files help store sensitive data locally, loaded by the application at runtime.

   bash

   ```bash
   pip install python-dotenv
   python
   ```

```
from dotenv import load_dotenv
load_dotenv()
api_key = os.getenv("API_KEY")
```

3. **Securing .env Files**: Exclude .env files from version control by adding them to .gitignore, keeping sensitive data secure.

Part 2: Building Interactive CLI Menus

Interactive CLI menus improve usability, particularly for multi-step applications or complex workflows. Libraries like InquirerPy facilitate intuitive menu navigation.

Creating Interactive Command-Line Menus with InquirerPy

1. **Setting Up InquirerPy**: Install InquirerPy to create prompt-based menus.

bash

```
pip install InquirerPy
```

2. **Building a Basic Menu**: Use InquirerPy to prompt users with a list of options.

python

```python
from InquirerPy import prompt

menu = [
    {"type": "list", "name": "option", "message": "Select an option:", "choices": ["Add Task", "View Tasks", "Exit"]}
]
answers = prompt(menu)
print("You selected:", answers["option"])
```

3. **Sub-Menu Navigation**: Guide users through multi-level menus by chaining menus and using their responses to control flow.

python

```python
def main_menu():
    menu = [{"type": "list", "name": "main", "message": "Main Menu:", "choices": ["Manage Tasks", "Settings", "Exit"]}]
    choice = prompt(menu)["main"]

    if choice == "Manage Tasks":
        manage_tasks_menu()
    elif choice == "Settings":
        settings_menu()
```

```
def manage_tasks_menu():
    # Define sub-menu options for task management
    pass
```

Using Keyboard Shortcuts and Navigation for Multi-Step Processes

1. **Keyboard Shortcuts**: Define shortcuts for frequently used commands. For example, assign "q" for quick exit or "n" to navigate back to the main menu.

2. **Breadcrumb Navigation**: For multi-step processes, display a breadcrumb to show the current position within nested menus, helping users maintain context.

3. **Feedback for Navigation**: Provide feedback as users move through steps, confirming actions or showing the current step:

python

```
print("Step 1/3: Select Task Type")
```

Developing Sub-Menu Structures for Complex Applications

For CLI applications with extensive features, breaking commands into sub-menus simplifies navigation and makes the application more intuitive.

1. **Hierarchical Command Structure**: Organize commands hierarchically so that users can navigate through levels to find specific functionality.

python

```
main_menu = {
    "Manage Tasks": ["Add Task", "View Tasks", "Delete Task"],
    "Settings": ["Change Theme", "Update Configurations"],
}
```

2. **Using Command Trees**: Define a tree structure for organizing commands and sub-commands, making it easier to manage complex workflows.

python

```
class CLIApplication:
    def __init__(self):
        self.commands = {
            "task": {"add": self.add_task, "list": self.list_tasks},
            "settings": {"theme": self.change_theme}
```

}

Part 3: Extending CLI Applications with Plugins

Plugins allow CLI applications to become modular and extendable, letting users add custom functionality without modifying the core codebase.

Adding Modularity with a Plugin Architecture

A plugin architecture allows users or developers to build new features and add them dynamically. This modularity is common in developer tools and larger CLI applications, making them highly customizable.

1. **Setting Up Plugin Folders**: Create a dedicated plugins folder where plugins can be stored and loaded at runtime.

   python

   plugins/
     task_plugin.py
     report_plugin.py

2. **Loading Plugins Dynamically**: Use Python's importlib to dynamically import plugins at runtime, based on files in the plugin directory.

python

```python
import importlib.util
import os

def load_plugins():
    plugins = []
    plugin_folder = "plugins"

    for filename in os.listdir(plugin_folder):
        if filename.endswith(".py"):
            spec = importlib.util.spec_from_file_location(filename[:-3], os.path.join(plugin_folder, filename))
            module = importlib.util.module_from_spec(spec)
            spec.loader.exec_module(module)
            plugins.append(module)
    return plugins
```

3. **Loading Plugin Commands**: Load plugin-specific commands into the main CLI application, extending its functionality based on active plugins.

Example: Building a Plugin Manager to Allow Third-Party Additions

A plugin manager centralizes plugin installation, activation, and removal. By handling plugins systematically, you create a seamless user experience for extending CLI applications.

1. **Plugin Installation and Activation**: Create a command to install or activate plugins directly from the command line.

   python

   ```
   def activate_plugin(plugin_name):
       if plugin_name in available_plugins:
           active_plugins.append(plugin_name)
           print(f"Plugin '{plugin_name}' activated successfully.")
   ```

2. **Plugin Metadata**: Define metadata (e.g., name, version, author) for each plugin, stored in a plugin manifest (e.g., plugin.json), making it easier to manage and update plugins.

3. **Plugin Command Integration**: When a plugin is activated, add its commands to the primary command structure, making them accessible as if they were core features.

This chapter covered three advanced features for CLI applications: secure authentication, interactive command-line menus, and extensible plugin architectures. By integrating these capabilities, you can build CLI applications that are secure, user-friendly, and customizable. Authentication ensures only authorized users access sensitive functions, interactive menus provide a streamlined navigation experience, and plugins enable flexible extensions for complex applications.

CHAPTER 25: CAPSTONE PROJECT – BRINGING IT ALL TOGETHER

The capstone project is a culmination of all the techniques and concepts covered in previous chapters, providing an opportunity to build a comprehensive, real-world CLI application from scratch. This project will combine multiple aspects of Python development, including data handling, web scraping, data analysis, and user interface design.

Project Outline: CLI Web Scraper and Data Analyzer

The final project is a CLI application that scrapes data from the web, analyzes it, and saves it to a file for further use. We'll walk through each component to demonstrate real-world use of key skills like web scraping, data handling, data analysis, user input handling, and CLI feedback.

Part 1: Project Planning and Requirements

Before diving into code, define the application's scope, its main components, and any dependencies.

1. **Application Overview**:
   - **Purpose**: A CLI tool that scrapes specific data from a chosen website, processes the data for insights, and saves it to a file format for analysis.
   - **Example Use Case**: Scraping recent articles from a news site, analyzing article data (e.g., word count, frequency of keywords), and saving results in CSV format.
2. **Project Requirements**:
   - **Libraries**:
     - requests for web scraping.
     - BeautifulSoup for parsing HTML.
     - pandas for data analysis and saving data in CSV format.
     - argparse for command-line arguments.
     - colorama for color-coded feedback.
   - **Basic Functionality**:

- Scrape data from the specified website.

- Analyze data for specific insights.

- Save processed data to a file.

3. **Project Structure**:

   o **Modules**: Organize functionality into modules (e.g., scraper.py, analyzer.py, saver.py) for modular code.

   o **Config Files**: Use a JSON configuration file to store customizable settings (e.g., scraping intervals, file paths).

Part 2: Implementing the Web Scraper

The web scraper component will gather data from a chosen website, parse it with BeautifulSoup, and store it in a format suitable for analysis.

1. **Setting Up the Scraper**:

   o Define a function to handle requests and fetch data from the target URL. Handle HTTP errors and ensure retries for robustness.

python

import requests
from bs4 import BeautifulSoup

def fetch_data(url):

```
response = requests.get(url)
if response.status_code == 200:
    return BeautifulSoup(response.text, 'html.parser')
else:
    print("Error fetching data")
    return None
```

2. **Parsing Data with BeautifulSoup**:
   - o Identify the target data elements (e.g., article titles, publish dates) and extract them.
   - o Implement error handling for cases where elements are missing or HTML structure changes.

python

```
def parse_articles(soup):
    articles = []
    for article in soup.find_all("div", class_="article"):
        title = article.find("h2").text
        date = article.find("span", class_="date").text
        articles.append({"title": title, "date": date})
    return articles
```

3. **Testing the Scraper**:
   - o Run the scraper and print a few results to verify the data structure.

python

```
url = "https://example.com/news"
soup = fetch_data(url)
articles = parse_articles(soup)
for article in articles[:5]:
    print(article)
```

Part 3: Implementing Data Analysis and Validation

Once the data is scraped, analyze it to provide useful insights.

1. **Setting Up pandas for Data Analysis**:
    o Convert the list of articles into a DataFrame to leverage pandas functions for analysis.

    python

    ```
    import pandas as pd

    def analyze_data(articles):
        df = pd.DataFrame(articles)
        return df.describe()  # Basic data overview
    ```

2. **Analyzing Data Attributes**:

- o Calculate insights like the number of articles, most common keywords in titles, and frequency of publication by date.

python

```
def analyze_titles(df):
    df['word_count'] = df['title'].apply(lambda x: len(x.split()))
    avg_word_count = df['word_count'].mean()
    print("Average Title Word Count:", avg_word_count)
```

3. **Validation and Error Handling**:
   - o Validate input data to ensure each article has required fields.
   - o Provide user-friendly error messages if data is incomplete or misformatted.

Part 4: Saving Data to a File

The application will save analyzed data to a CSV file for further use, making it accessible for future analysis.

1. **Saving Data as CSV**:
   - o Create a function to save the DataFrame as a CSV file. Add a timestamp to the filename to avoid overwriting previous files.

```python
python

import datetime

def save_to_csv(df, filename="output"):
    timestamp = datetime.datetime.now().strftime("%Y%m%d%H%M")
    filename = f"{filename}_{timestamp}.csv"
    df.to_csv(filename, index=False)
    print(f"Data saved to {filename}")
```

2. **Implementing CLI Arguments for Output Options**:
   o Use argparse to enable users to specify the output file format and location.

```python
python

import argparse

parser = argparse.ArgumentParser(description="Scrape and analyze web data")
parser.add_argument("--output", help="Output filename", default="output.csv")
args = parser.parse_args()
save_to_csv(df, args.output)
```

Part 5: Adding Interactive User Feedback

Provide real-time feedback to the user as the scraper and analysis tools run, making the application user-friendly and informative.

1. **Color-Coded Status Messages**:
   - Use colorama to display messages in different colors to enhance readability and guide users through each step.

   python

   ```
   from colorama import Fore, init
   init(autoreset=True)

   def print_status(message, status_type="info"):
       colors = {"info": Fore.CYAN, "success": Fore.GREEN, "error": Fore.RED}
       print(colors[status_type] + message)
   ```

2. **Loading Indicators**:
   - Display a progress bar for long tasks like data scraping using the tqdm library.

   python

   ```
   from tqdm import tqdm
   ```

```
import time

for i in tqdm(range(100)):
    time.sleep(0.05)  # Simulating task
```

Part 6: User Configuration and Customization

Allow users to customize settings, such as data source URLs, saving preferences, and analysis parameters.

1. **Creating a Configuration File**:
   o Store default URLs, output settings, and analysis parameters in a JSON or YAML file.

   json

   ```json
   {
       "url": "https://example.com/news",
       "output": "output.csv",
       "max_articles": 100
   }
   ```

2. **Loading Configuration at Startup**:
   o Use Python's json module to load settings, allowing users to edit the configuration file to adjust parameters without modifying code.

python

```
import json

def load_config():
    with open("config.json") as f:
        return json.load(f)

config = load_config()
url = config["url"]
```

Part 7: Testing, Debugging, and Optimization

Testing and debugging ensure the application runs smoothly under various conditions, with optimizations to improve efficiency.

1. **Testing with Mock Data**:
    o   Use mock HTML pages or API responses to test scraping functions, ensuring the application handles different data structures gracefully.

2. **Adding Unit Tests**:
    o   Write unit tests for each module, validating functions like fetch_data(), parse_articles(), and analyze_titles().

3. **Optimizing Code for Speed and Efficiency**:

    o Profile the code for bottlenecks and optimize functions where necessary. For instance, cache results when reloading the same data.

Final Thoughts and Extensions

The CLI Web Scraper and Data Analyzer capstone project is a comprehensive exercise that integrates key skills in web scraping, data analysis, and CLI interface design. This project provides a strong foundation for building complex CLI tools in Python, with further extensions like:

- **Scheduling Automatic Scrapes**: Use cron jobs or a scheduler library to run the scraper at regular intervals.
- **Extending Data Analysis**: Add sentiment analysis, trending keyword identification, or statistical summaries.
- **Enhanced Security**: Add authentication if the application connects to restricted APIs.

By completing this project, you'll gain hands-on experience and confidence in developing full-featured CLI applications that combine practical functionalities with robust code design.

www.ingramcontent.com/pod-product-compliance
Lightning Source LLC
LaVergne TN
LVHW051323050326
832903LV00031B/3333